T0137635

Gonna Be a Better Day

How to Try to End Racism

Fireman Bahb

Order this book online at www.trafford.com
or email orders@trafford.com

Most Trafford titles are also available at major online book retailers.

Print information available on the last page.

ISBN: 978-1-4269-2210-7 (sc)
ISBN: 978-1-4269-2211-4 (hc)

Library of Congress Control Number: 2009912306

Trafford rev. 06/04/2015

 www.trafford.com
North America & international
toll-free: 1 888 232 4444 (USA & Canada)
fax: 812 355 4082

About the Author

His name, Fireman Bahb, a proud American-American.

The world is on fire because of racism, and he's the only guy qualified to put the fire out.

With his glass half full and a positive mental attitude, come and take him as he is world.

An open book. Ha!!!!!

Dedication:

This is dedicated to anyone fighting…unnecessary wars and to everyone out there making an effort to erase hatred.

The Fireman knows that what we're asked to know can be a bunch of lies. We just can't live our lives alone no more.

So remember, if we strive for higher education, vote and wait a minute, by following these first steps, it's definitely gonna be a better day.

Check us out! Ha!!!

Contents

CHECK US OUT

I'm Keenan Smoove
I'm gonna make you move
With a New Style groove
Gonna make you move

I'm Fireman Bahb…B-A-H-B
I started believing in me….About the age of three
I know it took a little while….but worth the wait you see
Now I got a New Style….NSP

People wondering….who are you?
Call me Billy Who
When you wanna groove
I'm a make you move
Coming out of your shoes
New Style Grooves
Check Us Out!!!

I'm dedicated motivated under-rated never hating
Cause I got a whole lot of New Style Flavor!!!!
I'm a show stopper, mic-rocker, invented Hip-Hopera

Let me creep on in and join a friend
Me and Fireman back at it again
See we got this dream that we can't give up
Pumping funky hits yaw'll known as cutz!!!

The New Style Players are about to blow up!!!!
Who ever thought that we'd have sooo much?
Off the bus into a Cadillac truck
Here's a preview of some of our cutz!!!!

It's copy written haters so you know what's up.
Do your thang
Never Knew How Much
When I Awake at 3 O'clock
Call The Fireman
It's Gonna Be a Better Day
What we're asked to know like Back In The Day
When a Fool's Breaking Rules acting
Crazy!!!!

Chapter 1

What's up New Style?

My name is Fireman Bahb (pronounced Bob) and I have the audacity to believe that I was created to try to end racism in America and the world today, through word and song. In doing so I am going to approach this endeavor as if it is a reality show. In other words, anything is fair game, except for honesty. Ha!!!

Even though I am relatively happy about my life's accomplishments one of my biggest regrets will be that two of America's greatest heroes in the fight against racism Ms. Rosa Parks or Mrs. Coretta Scott King will be unable to read this. God blessed them both. RIP.

You may ask, what makes me think I'm qualified to be able to tackle such a huge obstacle, especially when it's tendencies have endured for so long, with no hope of ever being cured? Well, I'm an American-American citizen, and I have faith in the Most High. In other words to me, anything is possible. Ha!!!

Don't worry, I'm not going to turn you off with the blame game or that old "woe is me" crybaby crap. I have been very blessed to be able to keep my glass half full throughout my life's experiences, no matter how hard things may have gotten.

Believe me, I have had wayyy more than my fair share of troubles, so unfortunately, I'm an expert when it comes to keeping it positive.

But, that also doesn't necessarily mean that I am blind. Ha!!

For clarification's sake, here are some definitions that will come in handy, in no order of relevance pertaining to this songbook, taken from a 1969 edition of The American Heritage Dictionary of the English Language.

1. Racist-a person with the notion that one's own ethnic stock is superior. 2. Bigot-a person of strong conviction who is intolerant of those who differ with him in matters of race, religion or politics. 3.Discriminate-to make a clear distinction; distinguish; differentiate. To act on the basis of prejudice. 4. Prejudice-irrational suspicions or hatred of a particular group, race, or religion. An adverse judgment or opinion formed beforehand or without knowledge or examination of the facts.

Let's face it, racism, discrimination, prejudice, and or bigotry, do still exist today in our society, no matter how subtle or blatant. I view it as a sickness or disease that has a simple cure.

Well, maybe not so simple. Ha!!!

To discover my cure I had to think hard about the origin of racism in people and what it takes to actually WANT to be or become a racist.

To me it takes two major characteristics, ignorance and greed.

Lets face it; a person would have to be a big dummy to go through life consciously bragging about being some sort of a racist. This attitude is absolutely unacceptable, mainly as written law in this country. Simply stated, to go against the law means you are asking for trouble. That, to me, is an ignorant act, to go out into life ONLY looking for trouble.

Besides the reason for those feelings of racism are more than likely based on the fear of somebody taking something away

From you, or the bigger excuse....taking something away from your race?

Heaven forbid there could be the slightest reduction of the racists' so-called rewards. Ha!!!!

That is why I also label racists greedy.

Seems like it's always some sort of a complaint associated with taking something away from the racist like a job, a partner, political offices, classroom space etc., as some sort of an excuse or justification as to why racists feel the way they do. Never assuming responsibility for whatever bad things occur in their lives. It's always because of this Black guy or that Jewish guy.

Remember the lack of intelligence part of my definition.

Thank God we don't see too much of the KKK (Klu Klux Klan) anymore on television and such, talking about how inferior certain races are to the supreme white race. That, attitude in and of itself, shows nothing more than fear about their race being outdone by others.

Whisper whisper....

Huh....Who...What??? Tea Baggers?? Who are they??? Dude...can't you see I'm busy right now...anyway.

I'm sure people can recollect times when all the public ever heard from racist crybabies would be complaints about different groups and races threatening to catch up.

The racist response would be to use nepotism or cronyism in job hiring practices to keep "them" out. Ha!!!!

In other words, "they" (different people) could come in here and do a better job than the scared racist guy or girl.

Prejudice is not limited to country people from the southern states anymore. This attitude is prevalent all over the country, except for in California. Ha!!!!

If that were true then my cousin, Francisco "Boo" Hardy, would never have been chosen as the Long Beach Mississippi High School basketball coach in Long Beach Miss. or later, Harrison Central High School in Gulfport Miss.

Let's go teams!!! Ha!!!

Hurricane Katrina didn't discriminate when it came to its path of destruction, although, early during the aftermath, the way the situation in New Orleans was handled, it did seem to make a lot of people in the United States wonder about our then President's compassion.

Hey, don't go there!

Oh yeah, sorry…I forgot…no crybaby stuff. Ha!!!

Anyway, getting back to the southern mentality. I was watching the Larry Elder show one night and a black couple from the south were guests and they were talking about how they couldn't trust white people and that they will raise their child to "beware" of white people. Ha!!!!

Anyway, Mr. Elder then brought out a group of white female high school students who had put together a documentary about the people depicted in the motion picture, "Mississippi Burning." A story about three civil rights workers who were murdered in 1964 and the case was never solved.

It was an effort by Mr. Elder to prove to the black couple that all white folks aren't bad.

To no avail.

But, the black dude did get busy with a couple of the white girls. Just kidding. Ha!!!! JK

This Black couple, even though they were adamant in their beliefs, didn't come off as a threat or anything. They were more than likely trying to be on the safe side, you know, 'watching their back' based on our/their history.

That can, perhaps, be characterized as prejudice or discrimination. Not so harsh as a bigot or a racist. I don't envision the black couple with water hoses or ropes tied with the hangman's knot looking for some sturdy nearby oak tree. Ha!!!!

It did, however, remind me of the time I was a member of the audience on the Oprah Winfrey Show, when she held a workshop on racism. Mr. Lee Moon Wah produced a documentary called "The Color of Fear," about a retreat he scheduled for eight male adults of all different races to eat, sleep and live together for a weekend, to discuss race and experience their differences.

One white guy, Dave, was a special case because he was your typical person walking around blind, thinking everything's okay, until you're exposed to someone different like Dave was during the retreat.

There was this black dude, Victor, and fortunately he was extremely astute in being able to dissect Dave's negative comments to uncover his inadequacies.

Initially there was a lot of resistance from Dave who felt he was okay, because he had plenty of black friends and also had Native American artifacts in his home etc.

Remember nowadays it isn't cool to be a racist. Ha!!!

It took some doing but Dave finally had an awakening or a revelation when he said, "Maybe I do have a problem."

Bottom line, Dave was 'just confused,' he wasn't or isn't a bad guy, and it was proven after he discovered and accepted his fallacy.

Now Dave, I'm sure, is living a full, happy life.

The devil is sneaky ya'll.

And another thing Dave, as I inadvertently told you that day, "I got plenty of love for you my brother." Ha!!!!

Anyway, the black couple on the Larry Elder show, I would say they are also 'just confused' because anytime you reduce your claims to the color of someone's skin you eliminate any credibility in your argument because guess what, everybody's different.

In regards to race being responsible for any outcome we need to always remember that the basis of racism is a psychological hang-up and not biologically substantiated

Through my life's experiences it appears that to be a full blooded racist or bigot you would have to be an old timer.

Younger people aren't accepting racist notions as easily as

back in the bad ole days of "Jim Crow" and the "get to the back of the bus" era etc.

Unless you're a guy like personality Glenn Back you're more likely to be rejected than accepted today when people discover your bigoted beliefs.

Older cats had a better chance finding people weak enough to agree with their racist ideas back in the day, as opposed to trying to convince or recruit someone to be a bigot nowadays.

Whisper whisper....

Huh...what?? Tea baggers...again...well who are they?? Anyway.

I imagine it has to be pretty lonely for a person to actually choose living "the open racist lifestyle" today.

By the way, when the media does discover a racist, why do they get so much free publicity and I have to write a cotton-picking songbook to attain similar celebrity status.

What's up with that??? Not that I haven't had more than my fair share of brushes with celebrity.

Being a non-racist does have its small rewards, I guess, let's see I've personally met the artist presently and formerly known as Prince through my old dance partner, Cat Glover.

I'm sure Oprah Winfrey will remember me, even though I was 'only' in the audience that one day. I've even met Ben Affleck and Matt Damon before they were "Good Will Hunted." I also bumped into Mr. Diddy while in NYC for only a couple hours.

Not to mention countless other local Chicago celebrities in the music and entertainment industry I can honestly call friends, such as music producer/DJ/artist Steve "Silk" Hurley, Liza Cruzat an actress and model, or Tracy and Curtis Mayfield Jr. mainly because my dance/social club The Doctors started the legendary bi-level parties at my old High School in Chicago IL...Mendel College Preparatory.

And where would R. Kelly or his D.J. Wayne Williams be if I hadn't given Wayne and Jesse Saunders their first "big" gigs as The Chosen Few disc jockeys for my social club The Doctors?

I might as well include that if it hadn't been for friend Craig Thompson helping me give a blue jean party at a club called "The Warehouse" with Robert, Ziggy and Frankie Knuckles, then there probably would never have been the phenomenon known today as "House Music."

You're probably asking yourself, "What does all this have to do with trying to ending racism?"

Nothing, I just likes telling people this stuff. Ha!!!

Oh but wait a minute....Hmmmm...maybe it is pertinent because later on I will talk about how one person can make a difference in peoples lives. I often wonder if I was taken out of the Mendel/House Music equation like Jimmy Stewart in the film "It's A Wonderful Life" how different things would be today.

That's enough of me patting myself on my back. Ha!!!!

No, really, I want to show that the efforts of one person can truly make a difference in the world, no matter how that individual is perceived visually.

In other words, to look at me and or talk to me, you would never imagine these meager accomplishments.

I am reminded of judging a book by its cover. Ha!!!

Anyway, speaking of music, the theme of this songbook will center on songs that I have written or co-written with my friends. I selected material aimed at developing this story and soothing that savage beast called racism. All we have to do is apply the meaning of these songs to our everyday lives. Hint: read the lyrics along with the music so the message will sink in.

Yeah, I write songs, and you may wonder, "Why didn't he try to hook up with Steve Hurley, Prince or Mr. Diddy?"

Believe me, I tried, but it was all in vain. Then I had to suffer the indignity of seeing some of my best ideas duplicated 'successfully' anyway.

For example Robert Townsend used the term 'Hip Hopera' I coined for his production of "Carmen" starring the beautiful Beyonce.

I invented that word in the early eighties to describe the

unique style of music I write. Oh yeah, The Fugees, a pop/rock R&B group, even wrote a song titled Hip Hopera.

Perhaps they were searching for that 'identity' too.

Then I formed a singing trio called "All Tall" with Sal Munir, Tim Bolhar and myself around the same time, and we personalized a Hip Hopera version of the classic song "Sailing" by Christopher Cross. Alas the group broke up and what do you know, non other than Mr. Diddy himself covered the song.

Not to mention the Michael Jackson project "Jack and the Beanstalk" following the success of "Thriller" that never developed fully because it was a conflict of interest. You see I also wrote a masterpiece called "Jack'n the Beanstalk." (I've included a copy of the song as a bonus for you to hear) Ha!!!

Did I mention the rapper Lil Wayne came out with a song titled "Fireman."

Anyway, I'm not a professional solicitor and usually that is what it takes to be heard by the giants of an industry.

This songbook, however, should provide enough notoriety to create a buzz about my abilities as a lyricist/writer and believe me there are plenty more songs from where these came from.

Maybe Walt Disney will want to put this together as a Broadway musical AND on screen. Ha!!!

I'm old school. I feel there should always be a message in the music, which is why I felt this songbook concept will work.

So many times, people read my lyrics and comment on the social relativity of them or how they almost read like a poem.

That's basically how the idea originated for this songbook.

This songbook has a two-fold objective: 1. To try to end racism and the confusion of racism...2. As a feel good source to cultivate a positive mental attitude in all people, everywhere, the way nursery rhymes do for us.

Throughout my life I have always called myself trying to be thoughtful, kind and considerate of others. Helpful, maybe too much, and giving to anyone I thought I could help at the time, which is perhaps why I have never chased after many luxuries materialistically to speak of.

This is my ultimate gift to the world, this is what I think The Most High put me here to accomplish. I have always been able to communicate with people easily, effectively and humorously. I guess that's why I started writing lyrics in the first place, because I have a knack for putting words together well.

You know how people can go through life wondering what is their destiny? I KNOW this is my destiny, and well, I am NOT getting any younger, so, it's now or never. Ha!!!!

I believe there is a need for these songs, and if I didn't take this giant step putting together this songbook now, then I might've died, and they'd never have had an opportunity to be heard by the general public.

Leaving me with nothing but regret.

Since I can't get that elusive record deal, then my songs will get exposure this way, and one day, hopefully, Sir Elton John will actually want to sing "Lies" or maybe, Shakira will want to translate the song "No More" before I die. How about Usher singing "Just Can't Live." Double Ha!!!!!

The way I will format this songbook is to highlight different song lyrics that are written here, one song per chapter, that talk about trying to end racism and other foolish thoughts. Ha!!!

Then, I will associate that song to whatever aspect, of the songbook chapter's topic I want to highlight at that time. Ha!!!

For example, when all the people adapt to the ideas brought forth in this songbook I believe its "Gonna Be A Better Day."

Don't worry, you will quickly catch on.

Remember to read the lyrics as the song is being played so they sink in.

Music is so powerful, and by combining a melody or rhyme scheme with a potent or subtle message, it can do the work of a million foot soldiers. We've all heard that the pen is mightier than the sword and how any publicity is good publicity.

A lot of good, and bad can be done through the right medium.

I remember when I was at that Oprah Winfrey show, around 1994, how an entire audience came together for one day in an emotional, loving, learned type of setting that I'm almost certain has never been duplicated in the history of talk television. Ha!!!!

I'm sure people left that day wanting to help society get over their dumb hang ups about race in order for us to finally reach that next level of existence. We were an extremely diverse audience and caught a glimpse of what the world could be like when you walk around with blinders off, so that we can begin to judge people based solely on the "content of their character." Ha!!!

Who cares if you're a tall black dude with a funny haircut?

Wait a minute, that's sounds like me!!

This is an Oprah Winfrey inside joke; you had to be there.

Dear Oprah, we should have a reunion. Ha!!!

Anyway, one thing we were asked to do, during that workshop on racism, was to look around the huge studio and partner up with somebody who was different, someone you wouldn't normally approach socially.

Well I ended up with two wonderful white women as partners, (which was my dream come true...Ha!!!!) named Heidi and Debra.

When questioned by Ms. Winfrey after an exercise as to why they chose to do the 'exercise' with me, Debra talked all around the truth until finally it turned out to hilariously and simply be that she liked my haircut. Ha!!!

What a day!!

I made another friend that day outside the studio, a young Jewish lady, whose name escapes me, in town on tour with a dance troupe from NYC, and we ended up going to the Art Institute in Chicago for the Monet exhibit.

What a day!!

Oh, and for your information.... nothing happened!!! Ha!!! Although I have to admit she wasn't bad looking at all.

You know Ms. Winfrey made a comment that she stays away

from the topic of race for her shows because it never fails to get misunderstood some way or another, but this day she apparently felt very comfortable with our audience so she took a chance to make a point.

She asked our audience, "Did we feel America would ever have a black President in the United States anytime soon?"

I know…I know…Ha!!!!

100% of that audience agreed that this was not likely to happen, anytime soon. Remember this was in 1994 there about…Ha!!!

So Ms. Winfrey was able to make her point and move on, then, about a half hour later, this kobold white lady stood up and said she took offense to our implication that America couldn't have a black President.

I know…. I know…. Barack Obama…I know yawl… dang….Ha!!!! Moving right along….

Now, no offense to the little old white lady, bless her heart, but you could hear the whole audience kind of breathe heavy like "ohhh brother," Ms. Winfrey even said something to the effect of, "See, that's why I don't like doing this sort of topic."

It was funny, I have to admit, then Ms. Winfrey, to her credit, (big props) had to spend some time to try to get the woman to see where she was coming from. (Note: one of her producers even attempted to sort of point towards the clock as if to say, "let her think whatever she wants, we're off schedule" but good ole Oprah declared, "NO, I'm going to make sure she doesn't leave here with the wrong impression.")

It did take some doing, but you know what, the little old white lady finally said, "oh… well if you put it that way then you're right, America won't have a black President any time soon." Thus we were able to move on with our day.

Little did we know…Heh Heh Heh…? Yes We Can…Ha!!!! Anyway…

Kudos again to Ms. Winfrey, that brief interaction gave

me a lot of insight as to how difficult her job really is and her phenomenal success shouldn't ever be minimized.

Even though she never has enough good stories about the brothers on her show…except for maybe President Barack Obama. Just kidding…Ha!!!!

I don't want to spend the entire songbook talking about that Oprah Winfrey show (even though the experience is extremely relevant towards this effort) but I do want to talk about a different time when she decided to have a monthly show dedicated to the issues of race, motivated by the infamous Rodney King incident.

I want to say I got a lot of good information from watching those shows.

Please don't think I sit around the house all day watching talk shows, I don't.

I also like the soap operas. Ha!!!!

Anyway, I never would have learned, for example, about how Native Americans may resent being called, guess what, Native Americans, because it turns most would probably prefer we acknowledge whatever particular tribe they are from.

That is kind of like the way I feel we should always approach this whole race topic anyway, comfortably, on an informational basis, who needs more talk shows with the confrontational "KKK" guy trying to explain why he feels Blacks or Jews or whatever are inferior, and how somebody made up stories about the holocaust and slavery etc. That's going to go nowhere.

I even want to communicate and reach out to the Glenn Becks and the other bigots out there…if you aren't scared…hit me on face book.

I remember when the Oprah show traveled to Texas after an obvious racial-hate crime when three white men dragged a Black man, James Byrd Jr., to death behind a pickup truck.

When Ms. Winfrey discovered how infested the community was with racism she couldn't wait to leave that town. At least she 'tried' to help matters. In other words don't be afraid to 'try' to do the right thing.

Well this, again, is why I feel this songbook will be successful, because I am going to at least 'try' to get inside of anyone's head that is willing to listen and read. Hopefully leaving the so-called racists with enough logic to make a logical conclusion about bigotry, prejudice, discrimination and racism.

Perhaps I should add that everyone in that Texas town did not share the same negative racist ideas and some residents even admitted how ashamed they were to be associated with that ideology and stereotype. Ha!!!!

Again, a lot of times we are just confused.

I have had several jobs throughout my lifetime; you may even be surprised at how many of the companies I've worked with are in the upper echelon of Fortune Magazine's prestigious listing.

One of my many jobs was with thee Phone Company in Illinois now known as AT&T.

We were a union shop and one day during my lunch break a union steward, got into a debate "against" affirmative action with another employee originating from a talk show that happened to be on television at the time.

I stayed out of it, but I admit I was eavesdropping, until the union steward asked my opinion. Why did he do that? Ha!!!!

I was chomping at the bit to set the steward straight because as valiantly as the employee was trying she couldn't make the union steward see the continued need for any and all affirmative actions.

I have been thinking about these sorts of topics for a long time and presented my argument this way.

How long have we had this "dreaded" affirmative action?? Since1965 + or minus.

And what year is it now??? Fill in the blank. Now, how long have the benefactors (mainly black people) of this miraculous affirmative action been struggling?? Slavery in America began what, like 300-400 years ago??

So, even though it is one heck of a compliment, it always seems like white people (union steward) expect blacks to just snap out of our behaviors the day after we got that "magical" affirmative action.

We're supposed to become highly educated and successful people "all of a sudden" or normal parents (opposed to babies making babies left and right etc.) and move up out of these GHETTOS, and such, that are a BREEDING GROUND for negativity.

Most white people expect us black people to "miraculously" turn our lives around after we black people have been dumped on, whipped, raped and even lynched for almost 300-400 years. Ha!!!!!

Again, that's a heck of a compliment, we black people are resourceful, but let's at least give affirmative action a good 100 years or TWO before we go looking for these miracle results.

Black people have been dumped on for an extremely long time, even still today it can be argued, so it will absolutely take a little while for affirmative action to make a noticeable difference in all our lives.

We're good, but we're not THAT good.

The white union steward, after he picked his jaw up off the floor, exclaimed, "I never heard it put that way before."

I knew he hadn't and he probably never would have unless he bumped into me in his lifetime.

By the way (BTW) the same thing can be said of all these "Great Expectations" of now President Obama as to why isn't unemployment resolved or why hasn't the economy recuperated after 1.5 years in office.

That is another reason why I wrote this songbook. Ha!!!

I've got a knack for communicating.

I despair when I hear arguments about race and we black people represent ourselves like crybabies and make childish statements. I hate when we debate the advances we have made using the old us vs. the white man "holding us back" excuse.

My response will be, true some black people have successfully figured out how to maneuver in today's American society but we black people won't begin to love life fully until we "all" learn to love ourselves first. (See First Steps lyrics.)

I've worked for companies like Merrill Lynch, Time/Life Magazine, HBO, AT&T, Ameritech, SBC, Firestone, The Home Depot, The Chicago Fire Department and countless other individual entrepreneurial ventures.

I feel a lot of times we commit black on black crime by calling a person an Uncle Tom, for talking white or whatever, because 'Tom' has evolved to reach some level of success (depending on their definition of success) compared to whoever might be doing the criticizing.

When the truth could be they were maybe just lucky, and instead of spitting in the face of the blessing the said black benefactor 'Tom' chooses to continue to mature with grace vs. staying street.

Take for instance Allen Iverson, when he first came into the NBA he visibly had some sort of a rebellious chip on his tattooed shoulders, but look at him nowadays. He has evolved into a great team leader and someone we probably should even be proud of, maybe even a role model.

Now I live in Chicago, so I don't get to keep up with Mr. Iverson but he has made great strides with his image and his future, as a leader on and off the court, is a lot brighter.

On the other hand, we employed a guy named Ron Artest in Chicago for a little while, as a professional basketball player, where I developed a huge affinity for the guy.

I remember one game, the Chicago Bulls were in Los Angeles and Artest stole the ball from the Lakers Kobe Bryant 3-4 times in the closing minutes at such a critical juncture of the game I thought it was magic. (Houdini not Johnson) Ha!!!!

See I love defense, that's another story, anyway, fast forward to the fiasco where Ron hard fouled Ben Wallace in the closing minutes of the now infamous game between the Indiana Pacers and the Detroit Pistons. We saw a guy who perhaps was still clinging to his childhood, where that sort of violent behavior was acceptable or explainable, based psychologically from the unwritten laws of his old environment.

Maybe Pacer Ron Artest didn't realize it was time for a change in behavior and that he might need to carry himself a little differently perhaps. Especially since he's got this great job with the NBA, and all that goes along with it.

Well, it's a day late and a dollar short now because, as we all know, he got suspended for the remainder of that season. This sort of goes back to my affirmative action story.

We're good but we ain't that good. We still have a long ways to go.

Here's a guy, Artest, who was already wet from perspiration and he got upset because some one in the audience threw a beverage on him.

I'm not saying it's ok for fans to throw water on players before or after they are wet, like Gatorade at a football game on the coach, but I am saying black dudes in the NBA, and everywhere else, have to think before we leap, jump or react.

Maybe if Ron would have "counted to ten" he would have figured, let security handle it. He's bald-headed anyway (at that moment) it's not like they messed up his hair. It's not like he's got a Ben Wallace Afro or anything and gotz to go get his hair re-done. Ha!!!!

My main point is that here's a guy who may never need affirmative action. He is enjoying the financial successes of the American Dream, and perhaps still stuck with the ill after-effects of all the negativity of a society or race that has dumped on him and his old environment for so long that he obviously was struggling with this new lifestyle.

Hang on in there Ron; I am pulling for you "Tru Warrior" and God Bless you. Although that doesn't mean I want your team to beat the Bulls. Ha!!!!!

It is funny to hear white people judge him and other black men sooo easily.

I remember during the Olympics in Greece when the USA

Basketball team underwent way too much harsh criticism from our own country's sports columnists and journalists for not being 'team' oriented.

Forget about the fact the international rules are stacked against the USA.

I remember seeing the afore-mentioned Allen Iverson simply dribbling the ball toward our offense when he was literally mugged by an opponent near half court, but no foul was called.

It was also the first time EVER that I saw Tim Duncan react to a non-call or anything else for that matter. Tim Duncan never reacts to anything, not even winning a championship. Ha!!!!

It was very weird when our local sportscasters sounded salty after Iverson's buzzer beater to win a game. There were responses similar to, "I don't know what the team was so happy about." Things like that.

It totally reminds me of how Chicago-land residents used to cheer for the Boston Celtics over the Chicago Bulls even after Michael Jordan scored 63 points against the Celtics in the playoffs one year. (You know who you are)

Then we basically backed Scottie Pippen into a corner and demonized him for pointing it out. See, again nobody wants to be labeled or outed as a racist. Actions speak louder than words.

You may ask, "How does Fireman Bahb know that Chicago-land residents were cheering for the Bulls to lose, when it's supposed to have been a dirty little secret?"

Because in 1988 my father, one of my best friends, Brian Howard and I had finally found a venue where we could watch that 'satellite only' playoff game, after Mike's aforementioned heroics.

We went to the Ringside Sports Bar in Elk Grove Village, Illinois, just outside Chicago because you had to have cable at that time and it wasn't as available as it is now.

I remember distinctly how we hushed the crowd when we walked into a sea of Celtic euphoria being the only black people there. It felt like people were thinking, "How did they find out about this place?"

I knew about Ringside because I was working in the area at the time. Ha!!!!

Anyway, after the shock of these uninvited Black guys showing up the bar resumed to cheering for the Celtics, who went on to win the game (and series just in case you were wondering) when it suddenly dawned on me these people really didn't know anything about basketball.

All they cared about was which team had more white guys on it.

On my way out people were feeling our pain that the Bulls had lost, so I commented, "We'll get them next year."

That's when some dude opened his shirt, like Superman trying to find a phone booth, to display his Celtic T-shirt underneath and declared, "They got to get past these guys first!!"

Well since I know the game, I was instantly able to recognize that their basketball "gahds" (smile) were about to get their collective butts kicked by the 1988 Detroit Pistons and Isaiah Thomas. Ha!!!!

I can't wait for the next Olympics to see if....A. We put together a team representative of the challenge, so everyone can eat crow and B. hopefully all those then rookies like LeBron James, Carmelo Anthony and Dwayne Wade (not in any particular order...smile) come back to Team USA and just add Kirk Hinrich (best point guard in the NBA from that class... duhhhh) to the mix to get our gold medal back and make it a priority to never let it go again.

See I am, and always will be, a proud American, and when it comes to the Olympics you'll never get any notion that I'm cheering for another country (unless of course it's Rhythmic Gymnastics, man those girls look nice.) Ha!!!!

Speaking of being a proud American, what's up with this African-American crap? We, and you know whom I mean, ain't no African -Americans.

If we haven't had any recent close calls with a lion or a giraffe then you are, "surprise," an American-American. And for good reason too!!

I'm going to keep this simple…."Where were you born?" you were born in the USA then you are American-American. If you, your parents or grandparents etc were BORN somewhere else then you are _____-American.

My mother wanted all her kids to be born in Covington, La. My older sister was born in Louisiana and I just barely made it thanks to a harrowing ride from Mississippi to Louisiana after my mother's water had broken.

I am so grateful they made it or else I would have been born in the backseat of Cadillac, USA. Ha!!!

Unfortunately my younger sister didn't make it back to Louisiana and was the only one of us 3 children born in Chicago IL proper. (We don't hold that against you 'city girl.') Ha!!!!

Perhaps my mother did not want to endure another profanity-laced tirade from my father throughout the entire journey about how it didn't make any @#$%^& difference where I was born. (I'm putting it mildly to say the least, but I'm sure you get my drift…Ha!!!)

My point is this makes my older sister and I Louisianans and my younger sister an Illinoisan.

All three however were born in America. Thus we are American-Americans. Keep it simple people.

The sooner black folk start taking pride in their Americanism the sooner things will start turning toward our favor in regard to our struggles as a race.

I was watching an episode of "Trading Spouses," where Octavia, a Black mom from Harlem traded places with a white mom from a suburb.

During the show, Octavia ended up at a backyard Bar-B-Que one weekend and one of the white mom's relatives rudely asked her, what nationality she was. DUHHHHHH.

When Octavia replied "I'm African-American," the white

mom's relative PUSHED to know what PART of Africa did she originate from.

I'll never forget the look of pain and confusion on Octavia's face, as she replied, "I don't know."

Guess what America; none of us Black folk readily know what part of Africa we descend from, thanks to your white ancestors ripping us from our heritage. Don't get me started. Ha!!!

Anyway.

Wait a minute.

You know what, I will start.

Nobody appreciates how difficult it may be to not know your heritage, or "roots" as the white relative put it on Trading Spouses. Everybody, other than black folk, are walking around feeling wonderful about their family tree and how far back you are able to research your history and traditions.

Well apparently, black folk aren't so fortunate.

To be honest, what's so wonderful about knowing your great ancestor the plantation owner anyway?

We Black people were stripped of our history and now the so-called "intelligent people" wonder, "Why do Black people struggle so much, acclimating to 'our' society?"

Perhaps that was the master plan, to confuse Black people so much that one-day we Black people will need affirmative action.

Good plan. Ha!!!!

Anyway.

Oh yeah, one other thing about that Trading Spouses episode. The participants of the show were awarded $50,000 to be spent however the two moms chose.

This outcome is important because it really illustrates how, and I'm sorry to say, white people really just don't understand our predicament.

The black mom gave the white family the money for real time practical use. But, the white mom, after her "spiritual" black revelation, set up some stupid educational scholarships for the kids that can't be utilized for several years.

Wait a minute…am I criticizing education?

By no means.

It's just that the Black mom's kids may be lucky to be alive, let alone make it through school, to be able to make use of the white mom's decision.

The white mom is still confused. She still believes that "all they got to do is go to school" crap. That's what I call the 'Superman Syndrome' Black people are stuck with.

The network needs to re-do their reward and come up with something fair. I was totally left with a horrible taste in my mouth, and I'm sure I won't be alone after you readers review the episode.

Note: By no means am I saying reward that wannabe rapper instantly, who came across as extremely uncooperative. How about a couple of computers, a flat screen or some furniture for God's sake?? Anything other than that education pie in the sky that so many of our black people take advantage of every waking moment. DUHHHHHH

That's enough of the woe is me crybaby crap. Getting back to my American-American argument.

I happen to actually have some friends from Africa. Olive, Seth and Elike (pronounced El-eee-kay) are family, and they even have a distinguishable accent when they talk.

Sure they know English, but my point is they didn't get the accent on 47th and Cottage Grove. They are truly from Africa.

Me, I'm truly from 119th, also known as "the concrete jungle," or the wild-wild 100's."

Holla.

Sometimes, we as American-American folk may feel so cheated, due to that slavery backlash, that we sometimes jump at any opportunity for validation: The African-American label, Ebonics etc.

It's okay, to search for answers, as long as it doesn't come back to haunt us. Ha!!!

Candice Grube, a good friend of mine, brought something

to my attention while writing this songbook that I think goes unnoticed to the untrained eye.

She talked about the pain innocent white people may feel when black organizations call themselves Black. For example…. The Black Accountants of Hoboken, The United Negro Checkers Fund, or the African Bridge Club. Ha!!!!

Now, I never realized that these groups, while noble in their gestures, could cause a feeling of separatism to outside cultures, but apparently they can.

Let me explain.

Have you ever ridden on an elevator for example, and someone from another culture will start talking to his or her companion in a language other than English?

Am I the only one who can't stand that? Ha!!!!

Anyway!!!

I don't know about you, but I always think they're talking about me in front of my face, but they're trying to be slick and hide it by using their foreign language that I probably can't understand. Why do they do that?

Some people might even call that RUDE.

Anyway, the feelings that can evolve from a group being called the "Black Firefighters of Chicago," for example, can actually ruffle some feathers too. And this reaction should not be taken lightly.

Why, mostly because of our black folks history.

In other words, if anybody should provoke harsh thoughts about race relations it shouldn't be coming from black folks, ever, period.

I know, for the most part it is for a sense of pride of how far some blacks have come as to why these groups are formed, but in the spirit of LOVE maybe we should take this discussion to another level.

Now there's nothing wrong with the NAACP (National Association for the Advancement of Colored People), and the reason that organization was founded shouldn't be criticized too stringently about its chosen name.

And I love the acronym PUSH, People United To Save Humanity, or CORE the Congress of Racial Equality. These names were created during turbulent times; however, their creators were cognizant of everyone's feelings to not make matters worse. What's in a name? A lot.

See I will always believe that black people could never be prejudiced or anything like that. Witness how we welcome other cultures into the hood without any burning crosses etc.

So I believe strongly, and I hope I'm right, that the intent of these organizations is not to boldly ostracize society and publicly slap society back in the face as some sort of revenge on an elevator.

If so, this is stupid.

We might as well be keeping up with the racist Joneses.

If I am a graduate from law school, I hope I don't pigeonhole myself and call myself a black lawyer, and only associate with the Black Lawyers of America at the neighborhood Black McDonalds Owners Restaurants in my Black Fashion Designer Tailored Suit.... blah.... blah.... blah!!!! Do you get my drift?

Don't get me wrong, I love the educated brothers and sisters, but let's allow people to find out we're black AFTER they walk thru the door.

Don't give people the opportunity to turn away BEFORE they get to know you.

And be honest, you know some people would have a 'flying fit' if all of a sudden you heard about thee, "Whitest of the White-White Castle Owner's Association." Ha!!!

The only organization I can think of right now where the name does imply blackness, but shouldn't be changed, is "Soul Train."

See, really you didn't have to be black to get on Soul Train, you just had to have soul. (Remember the Asian girl from the Rick James video, "Super Freak?")

I will elaborate on this and other ideas throughout this

songbook, after all this is only supposed to be an introduction. So I'm going to close out by welcoming you to the world of "Hip Hopera" the new style of music I am sooo proud to say I am the godfather of.

This collection of songs and writings has an objective, to reach people and hopefully make them think about today's society and all peoples place in society.

Nobel Peace Prize…here I come…double Ha!!!!!

I couldn't just die and not make an effort to change the world so let's do this as I say in the Fireman Song, "Before I Die."

Check us out…Ha!!!!

THE FIREMAN SONG

Here I am
Something's funny about me
Here I stand…. still a mystery

There's a fire burning across the land
We need a Fireman
I'm gonna try because I know that I can
Put it out before it gets out of hand
Reach out my hand to you and you
See I don't care if it's black or blue
That is the reason we're confused

Before I die
Before I go
Tell the truth from a lie
I wonder if I'll ever know

The Fireman (love is growing up)
Will be there whenever you call (love comes from up above)
The Fireman
We won't be scared whenever you call
We're gonna be there and strong through it all

Why can't we all communicate?
Try teaching love instead of hate
Be ignorant or be educated
Figure it out before it's too late
This message is from me to you
Be careful what they're feeding you
I wanna plant a seed in you

I'm begging and I'm pleading

Chapter 2

Hey New Style

I hope you had an opportunity to read the introduction. If not I'll wait for you to finish reading the introduction, okay?

La-la-la-la-la-de-dah-la-la-lade-dah. Oh yeah, get a highlighter too.

You finished? Good!! Ha!!!!

Real quick, I want to give a couple of shout outs, one to my man actor Dennis Leary, for all he does in memory of his fallen firefighting family and his continuing efforts to bring attention to the risks of firefighting, even though we have never met.

Also to everyone who went to the Fire Academy with me in 1993, and worked Engine 63 and Truck 16's house in Chicago, I miss ya'll.

To everyone who remembers my old dance group "The Doctors" and partying with us at Mendel College Prep on the south side of Chicago and everywhere else back when I was in high school and college.

To everyone I know and everyone I ever knew a big "What's up!!"

To my nephew, I love you man.

To my family in Heaven, Oakland, Ca., the states of Mississippi, Colorado, Louisiana and elsewhere in the United States and let's not forget Venice, Italy. To all the girls I've loved before a great big shout out.

What's happening, New Style???

Now, as I said I'm Fireman Bahb and the world is on fire because of racism. I feel I am the only guy qualified to put the fire out. Ha!!!!

When I was employed with the Chicago Fire Department I learned that when someone is in trouble you do whatever it takes to help him or her through whatever particular "fire" they might be experiencing, period.

You don't just sit around and watch everyone else do the work.

I never thought about my ability to blindly risk my life, to help someone, until I joined that elite fraternity, and then that alarm would sound, not knowing where we would end up or what strangers we would end up trying to help.

We had a saying, "firefighters run into burning buildings, while the rats and roaches are running out of there, so who is crazy?" Ha!!!

Hey somebody has to do it, but it does take a "special somebody" to be a firefighter.

Little did I know what being a 'first generation' firefighter candidate actually involved? It turned out however that I was perfect for the task. And even though I am no longer there, I'll always be a fireman in my heart.

Make no mistake; I'm no longer a firefighter but I'll ALWAYS be a fireman.

You may ask, "What's the difference between a firefighter and a fireman?" The answer is…a paycheck. Ha!!!

I left the fire department DEPRESSED because my child's other parent took me through child support even though

I was giving her ungrateful posterior money for my child unsupervised.

I felt like I was being swindled and I was even pushed toward a marriage, even though the child is the result of a one-night stand.

Depressed, I coincidentally flunked my final drug test. I'm also probably one of a few candidates that had to take more than six drug tests anyway. I was a candidate for 2 years so I could've gone back to the CFD if I wanted to.

I didn't like the idea of child support labeling me a deadbeat when I was willingly and proudly giving money to the kid's other parent. I had to do some serious re-evaluations, especially after a fellow candidate got killed in front of our entire candidate class during an academy drill.

We were jumping into an air bag, while we were in the Academy, about to graduate with the rest of my Gold Star class.

The fatality happened right after I jumped into that air bag. This instantly revealed to me the difference between this career, and a so-called normal career at, say, the phone company, for example. Ha!!!!

When it became apparent I was going to get this 'great paying' city job, my kid's other parent ran to child support, like she had won the lottery or something.

To this day I can still see fellow Firefighter candidate Steve jumping from the practice facility and it still haunts me.

Long live Steve McNamee and may God bless you and yours. Ha!!!

Bartender!!!!!

Anyway, speaking of the Fire Department, in case you haven't figured it out yet, I'm a black dude, and in Chicago there was a myth that black guys had to struggle to make it as firefighters. Let alone get hired in the first place.

Rumors abound that the Department is prejudiced or that you have to know somebody to get hired. You know, that old "white man is holding us back" excuse.

Well for me, none of that was true.

I made a lot of friendships there that I will always remember, from all over the rainbow, and my experiences and accomplishments there, although brief, would probably compare to that of an old time Firefighter's resume. Ha!!!

Maybe even more so.

Let's see, while with the Chicago Fire Department, I made a video, our Academy class earned the coveted Gold Star Award, I fought 13 big fires, (countless meat on the stoves), and I was pictured in a national magazine for physical fitness representing the Chicago Firefighters (probably because I would always finish 1st-3rd in all our races we ran while in the Academy.) Ha!!!!

Least to say it was quite an experience that I will always cherish. It fostered a feeling of camaraderie I hadn't felt since my days back at Mendel Catholic an all-boys college preparatory high school on Chicago's south side.

Hey Firefighter Maureen McCarthy…. Ha!!!

Now SHE could/can run….Ha!!!!

The Fire Academy is a para-military environment so after graduation I felt like I could do anything.

That's when I wrote this "Fireman Song," about fighting racism.

I dreamed of a fire engine filled with 'love water', and when you turned on the hose, it would spray love all across the land, washing away the evil mentality of prejudice, discrimination, bigotry and racism,

I hoped to see it realized "before I die."

That was back in '94, and as we say, "It's gotten better, but there's still a lot of work that needs to be done."

The "Fireman Song" is my personal plea to everyone, asking us to rally round the 'guidon' or flag and simply communicate. Try to teach each other love instead of hate, be educated, don't be ignorant.

When we are ignorant, we turn ourselves into unaware victims, like Dave from the Oprah Winfrey workshop show. That's when smart people will laugh at you and your misunderstandings of reality.

So be careful what you're being fed.   Ha!!!!!

When a person is learning things from other racists perhaps that person should always inquire about the RELEVANCE of the lesson, to make sure there are no hidden agendas.

Make sure your innocence IS NOT an essential part of the racists' formula for success. In other words, the easier you can be manipulated the more likely you are willing to go along with the racists' agenda/foolishness.

I often wondered how Hitler was able to get soooo many people to blindly go along with such foolishness and evil.

Then I saw a documentary about his life and was astonished to learn things about the man I never knew before.

First of all, the guy apparently committed suicide.

That alone should tell us that deep down in his heart he knew he was doing something wrong. He wasn't really stable mentally in my opinion if he decided to commit suicide…just in case any readers still with us are out there who are pro Hitler and his ideology.

Not only did Hitler AND his wife commit suicide, apparently a contingent of his leadership also committed suicide when they were about to be defeated and caught. Ha!!!!!

I understand he even ordered the sterilization of over 400,000 Germans and that was considered good news!

Apparently, this brainwashing was aimed at German children around 10 yrs old and steadily intensified to ages 14 thru 18 yrs old, culminating in the form of a military draft, the ultimate allegiance.

To see the way the Nazis would aggrandize everything back then I must say, they resembled clowns. The uniforms were, however, quite stylish.

Hey I call it like I see it…Ha!!!!!

It always amazes me how gullible large groups of white people can easily go along with the crowd even though they look foolish and know that something is rotten.

Whisper whisper....

Huh...No I don't want any tea!! A teabag??? Wait a minute, can't you see I'm talking rather typing over here...anyway. Where was I?? Oh yeah.

A skeptic might say, "Yeah, but that was then and this is now," as an excuse that this sort of behavior doesn't go on anymore.

The problem is that it does go on and it is mostly unbeknownst to the white people who display and support these ignorant behaviors.

This continuously makes it hard to absorb these irrational behaviors of the lunatics by the intelligent and innocent bystanders.

Me. Ha!!!!!!!

So any attempts to get suckered society to adjust to these underlying problems are sabotaged because it all seems futile if you're not a member.

For example, when Scottie Pippen complained about the prejudicial treatment he was receiving from the Chicago Bulls home fans all the media wanted to do was to call him a crybaby. But, in fact, he was really onto something.

Remember the Celtics "fans" at that bar in Chicago-land?

Be aware that this stuff can and does actually happen and it is a serious problem.

I am happy to say that today I experience true Chicago Bulls home fans in almost all my travels around Chicago.

Maybe those six championship rings had something to do with it. Ha!!!!

When we don't get BOTH sides of a story, but we decide to pass judgment anyway, well then you tell me, "Who's the dummy?"

Why do we have to have a videotape of Rodney King almost getting killed before someone asks, "Can't we all just get along?" I wonder if we'll ever know the truth from a lie?

The truth is, it shouldn't matter what color someone's skin is to make a determination about one's character, personality, or their abilities, hopes, dreams, and desires.

But apparently it does matter.

Scottie Pippen probably thought he was helping a negative situation through exposure. He made an effort to show people the error of their ways.

Remember, one person CAN make a difference.

My objective for "The Fireman Song" and this songbook is basically the same: To let you know that everyone is in a position to take action. I want YOU to be that Fireman and try to make the world a better place, as much as possible, every day of our lives.

We all instinctively know the difference between right and wrong.

Sometimes, we recognize our wrongdoings instantly and as soon as we commit an act that we might not be proud of, we feel it.

We may put our heads down, laugh it off with a group or even acknowledge the error out loud.

Hey, we may be dumb but we ain't stupid…anyway nobody's perfect! Ha!!!!!

I always tell people about the difference between the U.S. soldiers who were photographed abusing prisoners of war from Iraq vs. the insurgents who would kidnap innocents and then behead them if their respective country refused to withdraw forces from the war for example.

The U.S. soldiers didn't cut anyone's head off.

This really may be an unfair comparison because the U.S. soldiers would never cut anyone's head off, although it was one of the supposed top arguments for the insurgent's behavior over how "bad" Americans are because we had prisoners also.

Anyway, my point is the big difference between them and us is the U.S. soldiers didn't cover their faces in those infamous photos.

I wonder why??

I think the answer is because the U.S. soldiers MUST not have thought they were doing anything wrong. Ha!!!!!

They certainly wouldn't have taken pictures to be used later as evidence against them, I hope.

The insurgents, however, must've known they were 'always' doing wrong because they 'always' had their faces covered up.

If they were so proud of their actions, wouldn't they want the whole wide world to see what they were doing and not hide their faces?

Or, were they well aware that they were breaking the law? Ha!!!!!

Remember, thou shall not kill is law all over the place.

The same can be said about the KKK guys and girls today who wear those sheets over their heads to hide from the repercussions of their actions. They KNOW they are wrong; what other excuse could they have to hide from society?

Even though a racist will chant, "white power" deep down in their soul they know they are wrong or else they wouldn't try to be so subtle about everything and strive to blend into a hoodless society.

All I can say is, before I die I want to tell the truth from a lie. Everyone should already know the difference between right and wrong.

This message is from me to you, be careful what they are feeding you. I want to plant a seed in you. I'm begging and I'm pleading.

The Fireman.... will be there whenever you call. The Fireman.... we're gonna be there and strong through it all. Ha!!!!

WAIT A MINUTE

Wait A Minute
Wait A Minute
Wait A Minute
(Fireman)
I got something to say
About
The problems, issues and concerns
(What)
Going on today
We're gonna (what)
Do it through our music
Changing the world when it's played
It's like medicine
If you choose to use it
It's gonna be a better day

Hold on for a second
If you've got the time
To check out this records
Rhythm and rhymes
(It's) a New Style of music
Make you listen with your mind
You will never accuse us of
Coming up with any old lines
Wait a minute

Note: there's nothing wrong with your system...the song sort of scratches at
the end.... Ha!!!

Chapter 3

What's up New Style?

Who does Bahb think he is? He doesn't have a talk show. He's not a Ph.D. All he ever did was win the dance contest on Soul Train with Academy of Our Lady's class of 1976 Valerie Dunn. Ha!!!!

Basically, Bahb is a nobody.

Well, so are the contestants on Survivor, the Apprentice or Big Fat Loser, pick any reality show, where the next thing you know someone's an instant celebrity.

All of the songs that Bahb has written haven't gone anywhere. Sure, his family and friends may think they are great, but ultimately, an artist wants the world to judge them.

Maybe that's why Bahb would go to the Cotton Club in Chicago on open mic nights. Perhaps he was tired of wondering if he could really sing well enough to entertain a crowd. Or was he just fooling himself?

Well, it turns out people loved his rendition of the James Taylor classic "Shower the People" even though the Cotton Club was mainly a jazz club.

He actually became somewhat of a regular there too, until he took the bad advice of a "friend" who told him to stop singing live there, and record in this certain studio, for a fee. Ha!!!!

All his efforts were in vain.

Wait one Cotton-Club-picking minute! Double Ha!!!

Bahb wanted to quit, even though, in his heart, he knew he had enough talent to succeed as a songwriter because of his knack for communication.

So he continued to wander about like a songwriter with his head cut off.

After years of going from one studio to another, one band to another, Bahb gave up on his dreams about the music business, until a friend, Keenan "Smoove" Pettiford, introduced him to this guy named Billy Who.

Well, Billy Who turned out to not only be a great rapper but also had the ability to create hypnotic beats. The three of them collaborated on a couple of ideas and next thing you know The New Style Players were born with a new style of music to make you listen with your mind. Ha!!!!

Billy Who would always comment, about Bahb's ability to come up with lyrics, almost at the drop of a dime, lyrics that were not only catchy, but for lack of a better word, DEEP.

Well, Bahb had something to say about a lot of things, for example.... black Americans calling themselves African-Americans.

Wait a minute.

Bahb thinks that's wrong! He thinks it will prevent the Black American population from ever taking pride in THIS country that was built off our ancestors' blood, sweat and tears.

True, black folk are ultimately from somewhere in Africa, but unless you are "Roots" author Alex Haley you probably will have a relatively hard time figuring out what part of Africa your family tree is rooted.

Bahb strongly believes that this is a way for Black America to begin to right the wrongs of slavery and claim what is rightfully ours. A beginning to an end.

Wait a minute. Ha!!!!

Black folks should embrace America, not that there's anything wrong with Africa; it's just that Bahb feels we have to crawl before we can walk.

To Bahb, rallying around an African flag, is a noble gesture, but it confuses American Black people even more. One of the first steps by blacks toward receiving reparations should be to take pride in this country, mainly cause it's all we got, God bless her.

You know, if you look at it, with the exception of all the tribes like The Sioux or The Cherokee Nations, Black people are really the truest of American citizens. Ha!!!

Think about it, most people are rather proud to proclaim their heritage, whether they are Italian-American, Irish-American, Chinese-American or Latin American, for example.

Black people, however, can't as easily trace the original traditions of our true African culture. That's why I feel embracing a more recent and recorded American history is a respectable place to start.

So, not to sound insensitive to this plight but when you got a lot of lemons, it's time to make some lemonade. Ha!!!!!

Wait a minute.

In other words, begin to make the most of the situation.

Sure, Blacks can talk about reparations. Maybe free education or release the overwhelming majority of black males from jail over those silly non-violent drug convictions.

What did he say??

Maybe even make it legal for blacks to get high on drugs and release us from prison, since we Blacks have such a heavy burden on our shoulders from all the years and years of struggle we have had to deal with.

Yeah right.

Just making sure you're not falling asleep out there!
Anyway, that's not Bahb's job to talk about what reparations we should actually receive. Bahb's jahb is to try to end racism.
This New Style Player wants to "do it through his music," changing the world when it's played.
Hold on for a second, it's gonna be a better day.

Wait a minute.

The Fireman has got something to say about the problems, issues and concerns that are going on today.

Hey New Style…. I'm Baaaaaack

Have you ever been in a group situation and the conversation would turn to some commonality that made everybody want to share his or her two-cents?
Race is usually that sort of topic that will get everyone's dander up.
Perhaps that's what was so intriguing to me, to make me want to know more about people like Ms. Ida B. Wells and Dr. Martin Luther King Jr. since the subject of racism dominated their lives.
Or, why I HAD to be at Oprah Winfrey's workshop on racism.

I became obsessed with attempting to find a way to solve this problem of racism that I consider to be a disease and a disability.

Everybody has different concepts about race relations that are all over the spectrum.

Debate is not only healthy, but I want to encourage it, so that sooner or later we will eliminate the offensiveness of the topic.

Have you ever seen any comedies or parodies where a white person will accidentally say to a black person, "You people?"

He may as well have just used the dreaded "N" word.

Its positioning is what can make it offensive, not when Adam Sandler was on the airplane in the film "Anger Management." That was not supposed to be an intentional insult to the airline employee, it was meant to simply designate the mis-management of the airline only.

Watching this program "Black/White" there were some people who were involved in an experiment, disguising themselves as their 'opposite' race.

A white woman during a complimentary poem made the horrible mistake of calling human beings "creatures." It caused an uproar amongst the Black cast members.

Here we go again.

Figure it out people.

Unfortunately, we are on such an edge that "you people", or "creature," may ALWAYS be taken the wrong way. I wonder how that ever got started anyhow?? Ha!!!!

Oh well, speaking of the "N" word, if someone ever says that to me TODAY in an effort to make me angry, I truly believe I will laugh at him or her for being childish.

Don't get me wrong if I never hear it again it will be too soon. Anyway.

Our guitar player and co-writer John is not black, but there had been plenty of times when he would slip and call someone that "N" word and we would laugh about it.

John explained the only reason he said it is because he's heard other members of New Style Players say it to each other and it just slipped out.

Wait a minute.

No offense was meant and none was taken. I love you John. (We ain't gay or nothing. John is married with three kids. Not that there's anything wrong with being gay, see Seinfield episode.) Ha!!!!

In other words, stop the madness.

I know that I might be missing something when it comes to this debate. Again, nobody's perfect.

So if you want to share your two-cents, there will be information available how to contact New Style Players, to be reviewed for discussion. Perhaps a Fireman Bahb web page, blog, face book or something.

Wait a minute.

If YOU'VE got something to say about the problems, issues and concerns going on today then holla back!!! Ha!!!!

Become a fan of Erase Hatred on facebook....;0) Ha!!!

WHAT WE'RE ASKED TO KNOW

Growing up sometimes is tough
Trust deep inside your heart and mind
Hard to decide which way to go
Can't explain…what we're asked to know

My fingers are crossed I won't get lost
Still here I go on this bumpy road
I won't be scared, just be prepared
Never know what the future has in store

Can't explain…what we're asked to know
It's hard on your brain…what the future has in store
It's hard to believe…because you've heard it all before
It's not important compared to what we're asked to know

Live and learn to wait your turn
Don't build a bridge just to see it burn
Birds and Bees in a forest full of trees
Hard to believe…because you've heard it all before

Look both ways and then decide
Can I follow or should I guide
Casually or carefree
(Always) Comes back around…to what we're asked to know

Chapter 4

What's up New Style?

Do you have kids? Are you a child? Either way we human beings have a huge responsibility. The world is in our hands and our most High, our higher power, wants us to live in peace.

I know we have war and we have murder, we have love and we have hate. I have come to the conclusion that we are everything that we are, based on the CHOICES that we have made throughout our lives. Ha!!!

That's right, we actually do govern our lives as adults, as children, as Black people, Asian, Irish, everyone. We are in total control of our lives. Isn't that empowering?

It should be.

To know that we truly have total control over our destiny is also comforting TO ME because I was raised very well by my parents and my extended family.

For someone like me, it's always puzzling why people, me included, choose to commit wrongdoings, when they know that decision will only lead to trouble.

Am I coming through?

Don't get me wrong, I've made many mistakes in my lifetime, my point is they were "MY" conscious CHOICES.

CHOICE is really huge when we think about it.

Wouldn't it be wonderful if we could tell the future and shape our lives? Well guess what…. we can!

How?

By the CHOICES we make. Ha!!!!

For example, if we CHOOSE to study hard, do our homework, and stay out of trouble, our lives should be rich.

If we CHOOSE to study racism and hatred then your lives will be confused.

The CHOICE is always ours to make.

With the possible exception of the learning disabled, and even they are often capable of discerning the difference between right and wrong, we are always to be held accountable for our actions.

This is "what we're asked to know."

I have a friend who has a kid. I would say "supposedly" has a kid because my friend has not experienced one solid day of respect from this child since the kid was old enough to disrespect him. What kind of child-parent relationship is that? Horrible, to say the least.

Even though they do not live together and he chose not to marry into the other parent's family, he is still the male parent.

You can imagine that not wanting to marry the female parent didn't go over too well.

Who cares, after discovering an enormous incompatibility, that marriage would've been adding insult to injury.

As a result the kid has been coached by the female parent, and her extended family, to disrespect the father as much and as often as possible.

For example: I…I mean he made up his mind a long time ago, that if and when he were to ever father any children, he would want to be referred to as "father" as opposed to being called "daddy."

A simple request, right? Ha!!!!!

Wrong, this kid is pushing nineteen years old and has never abided its father's wish. Blatant disrespect.

Now some people may have their opinions about this father.

Is he paying child support? Is he ever around emotionally for the kid? What's the big deal anyway? There must be a reason why the kid continues to disrespect the father. Let the kid call him whatever the kid wants to call him.

All that is fine for speculation, but my simple point is, why can't the kid follow its father's instructions? It's because the female parent and her cohorts kept telling the kid to call him "whatever."

They are raising the kid to behave this way.

Do you remember that time YOU tried to call YOUR parent by their first name and they instantly corrected you?

That was improper. We've all been there. There was no problem afterwards, was there? As a child, you were innocently mimicking what every other adult was doing. Calling your parent by their first name.

Now, fast forward to a racist adult who has children.

You know, the parents who are brainwashing their kids to call Blacks the "N" word or Hispanics the "W" word etc. do you see the correlation?

My point is kids are vulnerable to adult leadership, and the things adults teach them will be with them for a long time.

It would probably be smart to make sure that the kids don't have any regrets about something that was forced upon them as children by the so-called adults. Ha!!!

I am...I mean my friend is extremely disgusted with his child's attitude about life and the child's behavior towards him, even though he knows the kid was trained to think whatever way about him.

A lot of people have said it's not the kids' fault; rather it's the other parent who is responsible for coaching the kid to act that way towards the father. I have to disagree.

See even as children, we are exposed to circumstances when a CHOICE is going to have to be made. We innately and instinctively experience familiarity with the difference between right and wrong at an early age, it's very simple.

Ask children: Is it O.K. for one parent to make another parent cry? Is it O.K. to torture an animal? Is it all right to kill another human being? What about stealing or lying or cheating? Do we have to constantly be reminded which way to go?

The kids' excuse for not addressing the parent as father was, "I don't have to, I can call you whatever I want to." Ha!!!!

Well I disagree strongly so I'll just continue to pray for the kid and one day perhaps the kid will look at things differently. I hope the kid reads this one-day. Sometimes things are clearer from the outside looking in.

I'm not going to waste too much time talking about his little "ungrateful ingrate" this songbook is on a greater mission to better the condition. The kid will have to work it out the best way it can. God bless em', I'm pulling for us...I mean them to work it out one day when there is trust there.

All right, all right, the "friend" is actually me.

At first I was being sensitive to my child's plight, but as I said, to this day I am still being horribly disrespected.

Anyway, "What We're Asked To Know" is a song for all the children of the world.

I am reminded of a time when I was in high school, oh yeah, still a child, and my social club "The Doctors" was holding a basketball game, and sock-hop party in Mendel's gymnasium.

It was a big gathering, as usual, and for the sake of explanation it was like a "local celebrity game" but on a small scale about 4-5000 people were in attendance.

The team we were playing was also 'somewhat' popular (I got to get my digs in when I can.... Ha) and we really didn't have too many H.S. basketball players on either team except for Ray Rhone from De La Salle H.S. on the opposing team "GQ", and

Rory Brown committed to St. Francis H.S. on our team "The Doctors."

True, I love the game of basketball as much today as I did then, but I never played on an organized team before, in an environment such as this with a big crowd, referees etc.

I went to a lot of trouble to make sure I didn't embarrass myself by arranging for some private coaching weeks before the game from Rory's older brother Rodney who was also a former catholic-league all-star. Ha!!!

Although we lost the game we faired relatively well. But something happened during the game that is relevant to this chapter.

Imagine a child is going about his merry way under the impression he is doing the right thing. He may have been preparing, like me, to wait for the right moment to jump out there and spring a cat-like move on everyone to impress all the people around him or her.

Well I had been contemplating this fast break in my head that I would leap on if given the chance during the game. It was sort of a behind the back, through-the-legs lay-up that was you know, show time.

Unfortunately, I have never been able to easily dunk a basketball even though I'm 6'6" inches tall. (I finally feel safe telling this since I don't play as often as I used to) Ha!!!!

So I learned this amateur move and practiced with all my might until I got it perfect. I couldn't wait until I could spring the move on the unsuspecting crowd, thus earning the coveted reputation of being someone who can play basketball and subsequently get picked up in the first round of pick-up games. Which, by the way, is a big deal.

Well that moment arrived on an intercepted pass I caught and boy was I in Heaven.

I was grinning from ear to ear, shaking and baking all the hands waving at me, attempting to stop me as I gingerly maneuvered through what seemed like eight or nine guys trying to stop me.

The crowd was yelling at the top of their lungs and there was so much adrenaline rushing through my veins I was in another world, with my eye squarely on the prize, to score.

Nothing else was important; I couldn't see anything else, feel anything else or hear anything else.

Too bad.

Maybe I would have heard the entire gym yelling, "Bahb, stop, you're going the wrong way!"

That's right, I was going the wrong way.

Oh my God.

Was there a foxhole I could hide in? Did anybody bring any sunglasses for me to hide behind? Nope. Boy was I embarrassed! Not to mention the aftermath of ridicule I had to endure, for like, the rest of my life. Ha!!!!

I still smile every time I think about it. It was an innocent mistake and basically the, 'as usual, nothing new' story of my, Andy Hardy life.

No wonder it felt like nine guys were trying to stop me. It WAS nine guys trying to stop me.

It's just that I was so caught up in that fantastic move I learned, that I couldn't wait to show it off. I guess that is why I was deaf to all the shouting. Ha!!!!

I say this to make the point that children are also anxious to show what they have learned to their parents and other people.

In their exuberance, a child taught to be a racist may never hear the majority of the general crowd shouting, "STOP, YOU'RE GOING THE WRONG WAY!"

One of the things my father taught my two sisters and I growing up is that "money is man-made." That enabled me to grow up unimpressed with the so-called riches that so many people have been taught to crave.

I was, am, and always will be able to go throughout my life without any temptation to do whatever it takes "for the money."

That was a great lesson for me as a child and it proved to be a great assist toward achieving the successes I experienced later on in my young life and as an adult.

For example, even though I wished for a career in the music business, it never happened. Did I go out and start robbing, stealing, cheating or killing out of frustration/spite?

No. I bit the bullet. Besides, I'm not a coward. At least I hope I'm not.

Remember, in my mind's eye, my glass is always viewed as half-full. Ha!!

Even after my "chum" from high school stole everything from my parents legacy and me. I still CHOSE happiness.

Well, as happy as a brother can be, being dang near broke and practically homeless. Ha!!!!

Anyway.

To all the children, and I guess adults too, when you are faced with decisions, no matter what the circumstances, try to CHOOSE the right decision.

Don't take the easy way out, that's not always the right CHOICE.

It's funny sometimes what people believe and act on.

We have to be careful with our decisions, be very careful. There might not be anyone trustworthy around to tell you when "you're going the wrong way." Ha!!

For example, it would have been easy for me to harbor feelings of hatred, anger and revenge against that 'friend' who stole from me.

Wait a minute; I do hate him, I am angry. Ha!!! JK

My philosophy is to keep on stepping, it'll get greater…later.

I'd be doing myself a great disservice if I walked around with my lips stuck out all the time, whenever I was unable to get my disappointments off my mind.

I admit, I have had way more than my fair share of pitfalls to overcome, but I believe as we all should that if it doesn't kill you, it will only make you stronger.

So now, I spend a lot of time at the gym working out. (Ha.... get it, stronger, I wish...see love handles) Double Ha!!!!!

You may ask, "How do we know which way to go?" Well if you don't know, then you better ask somebody! Ha!!!!

Not just anybody either. Find a teacher, a minister or a police officer, maybe the proprietor of the neighborhood candy store. Try a neighbor or better yet you may be lucky enough to have an entire audience screaming at the top of their lungs at you about which way you should be going.

Find anybody who can be objective.

Just don't ask the 'friends' who fill our heads with nonsense like my daughter's other parent.

I'm sure you'll know when you find someone you can trust, if not, when all else fails there's always you know who...Pastor Joel Osteen. JK....then again maybe I'm not. Ha!!!!!

You know I mean Thee Most High, your higher power, as long as love is in the formula you'll be okay.

Read YOUR bible as a manual for guidance, and instruction on how the world is supposed to be.

I can't explain.... what we're asked to know. Ha!!!!

FIRST STEPS

Have you ever been in love with somebody
that hurt you bad and made you feel you're no good?
That hurting feelings from the loving you're giving
cause you don't love yourself the way you should.

Then you wake up!
Look in the mirror to find you've been lying to yourself all the time.
You thought life was about making other people happy
while number one's priority on THEIR minds.

Loving your self's first steps to loving someone
Loving your self's first steps to loving someone
Follow this rule and your life will be fun
Loving your self's first steps to loving someone

How many of you
out there can relate to this.
Do you put others above you
knowing that you're taking a risk?
Family friend or a lover you say nawww
they'd never do that to me.
Next thing you know their scheming will leave you
walking around in disbelief.

The moral of the story
Is to never ever forget who's number one (that's you.)
Finding true love will be the least of your worries

Loving your self's first steps to loving someone

Chapter 5

Hey New Style

Maybe it's about time I get into the real nitty-gritty of how I think we can rid this country and the world of racism.

As I said earlier, to discover the cure you have to have an idea of racism's origin.

Remember ignorance and greed? These qualities may be somewhat simple to describe but they are not simple concepts and may be even more difficult to attain.

These are learned traits.

Or should I say "unlearned" with respect to Ignorance.

The American Heritage Dictionary defines ignorance as "Without education or knowledge." You can also be unaware or uninformed.

This does not necessarily have to be construed as an insult but it should be more of a red flag with respect to racism.

Should one find your selves in the predicament of being attracted to racist behavior, perhaps you need to look at yourself in the mirror a lot closer than you have been.

In regards to allowing ourselves to become racist there is also the tendency to be somewhat of a follower.

I know, get it straight, either you're ignorant or you are a follower right? You may wonder, "How can a person LEARN ignorance (to be that said-follower) AND be ignorant at the same time, since ignorance basically means the inability to "learn?"

Wait a minute,

I got something to say.

The information that a racist gathers is generally taught to an individual. It's not like you're born a bigot. People are coached or taught to hate. Some may even say brainwashed. Ha!!!!

Anyway.

Without trying to sound contradictory, the ignorance factor for racists doesn't mean you are incapable of learning, it means you are CHOOSING to ONLY learn the bad things about life particularly when it comes to trying to be a racist.

That to me is ignorant.

Remember in school when your teacher would tell you something and if it didn't make sense to you, what would you do?

Raise your hand and ask for an explanation, right?

Okay then, the explanation for the development of a racist can be based on that certain individual never questioning the teacher.

Imagine, never raising your hand. Ha!!!!

Just follow along, do what I tell you to do, even though it may not make much sense to say…antagonize Jewish people for example.

Yet and still the racist followers are gullible enough to act out whatever instructions are given to them.

That person is ready, willing and able to accept everything the teacher is feeding them about society as the gospel truth. No challenges, just blind allegiance.

Remember the old expression, "if so-and-so said jump off a bridge, would you do it?"

Whisper…Whisper

Dude there you go again about those tea baggers....What is the deal? Anyway...Humph!!

Well in the case of the bigot, I'd be inclined to believe that he would jump off that proverbial bridge.

If the KKK guy told them to, that is. Ha!!!!

A lot of my determination is based on a documentary that clearly depicted how Adolph Hitler was able to get away with convincing millions and millions of people to believe in utter nonsense.

What was really the most shocking is how gullible people can be to such an obvious, blatant, gigantic wrong.

Even though we may speak a different language, people are BASICALLY the same all over the world.

Surprise!!

That's right.

We are all basically the same. Ha!!!!

This is why I have always been able to approach all kinds of people on all different levels.

I might describe myself as very approachable and relaxed in society's varied climates.

I decided to be educated at an early age. Why, I don't know.

I guess I figured that the only way to stop racism was to try to get to know people.... all people.

As many people as possible. Ha!!!!

That's what I remember sharing with my partner Debra during the Oprah Winfrey workshop on racism.

I told her," Don't go through life as a victim, when you close yourself off from people you're not allowing yourself to grow. Think of it like this.... imagine an expressway, (it appears some people also refer to them as highways...ahem) now imagine all the cars on the expressway during rush hour in Chicago...it's packed right?"

"Now I want you to realize that everyone in these cars have lives. Everyone is different. And everybody may be searching for something. They may be searching for the truth. That's pretty awesome, right?"

"Well what if you had the chance to meet someone with "The Answer," and you passed it up because of some foolish belief.

Well, now you are a victim."

It must have made an impression, because after the show I remember Debra telling me that she won't raise her kids to be victims.

Hold on Debra…there are some Black people I do want you to keep your kids away from. Ha!!! We'll talk about that later.

This songbook is about trying to end racism.

Holla back Debra AND Heidi for that matter…new style.

Now, where was I….oh yeah, the racist.

The racist students tend to travel safely in packs of people who claim to believe that skin color determines a person's worth.

They may even hide out on the Internet and e-mail each other with updates about books, rallies or racist churches where they can meet in secret.

To the viewer it would appear they are a strong group of people.

In actuality, I'd be forced to call them weaklings, not as an insult, but more so because they are emotionally or psychologically weak. Ha!!!

They are actually lost souls that we really should, and probably need to, pray for. They may view themselves as porcelain, where everything rolls off their backs.

In actuality they should be held more accountable for disrupting society for no good reason.

Everyone loves a just cause but nobody likes an action "just because."

Whisper…Whisper…

Dude, I wish you would stop doing that

There's a song from the film "Urban Cowboy" starring John Travolta, Debra Winger and Scott Glenn. "Looking for Love in all the Wrong Places."

Love is precious and should be handled very carefully and delicately.

To me the racist student is looking for love, but in all the wrong places. To me, they crave some sort of acknowledgement or acceptance that they may feel is lacking in their existence. Ha!!!

Sometimes, all they may want simply is a friend.

A comrade or confidant they can trust.

But, in a moment of weakness, the student was easy prey to the vulture like mentality of the racist devil.

As usual the devil was lurking around, waiting for some chump to fall for his ridiculous fairy tales about how horrible your life is, in hopes you will jump onto his bandwagon of merry Republicans...I mean racists.

The devil is lonely ya'll. Ha!!!

Why else did he trick Eve and Adam in the Garden of Eden with that apple?

He was lonely and wanted some company.

I want the racist student to see him or herself naked, just like Adam and Eve did, after they realized they had messed up big time.

It's actually somewhat similar in circumstances.

You know, the Adam and Eve story, and the revelation of the racist.

Remember, being conned into thinking it is okay to hate anything, let alone a race of strangers, should be a very eye-opening experience.

All hail the racist king with no clothes.

How are you going to hate someone solely based on the color of his or her skin? It's already sad that you worked up the gall to hate somebody in the first place.

Remember, the Lord don't like ugly! Ha!!!

Perhaps I've said enough about the "ignorance quotient" part of my formula, let's discuss the greed quotient now.

That same Dictionary I referred to earlier defines greed as a rapacious desire for more than one NEEDS or DESERVES, as of food, wealth, or power; avarice.

Just for your information, "rapacious" means taking by force; plundering, and "avarice" means an extreme desire to amass wealth.

The racist teacher, or the devil, has to have a "what's in it for you" reason to convince some people to join his band of merry bigots.

For example he may try to instill a fear that your race will disappear if you date outside of your race, or fear that a race will take over if "they" keep climbing that social ladder.

All this is doing is relying on a fear based upon the belief that you are foolish enough to 'greedily' want everything for yourselves. Also known as "no competition" or the plundering of a race for selfish gains.

I am reminded how I allowed a high school 'friend' to live with me while he was getting his life together, only to later find out he stole my identity to commit all kinds of fraud that resulted in the loss of the house I grew up in, my brand new pick-up truck was repossessed, and several thousands of dollars were stolen through credit cards and my credit union, all so he could get high on drugs at my expense.

To me, that was extremely greedy. The 'friend' was under some delusion that somehow the house my parents had worked so hard for, was willed over to him somehow.

So he stole my identity and began getting all kinds of loans in my name until the police caught up with him. Thank God, or else I would be writing this book from prison for murder. Ha!!!!

I have spoken to the jerk, and I guess I would like to hear his excuse for not wanting to get a normal job, like everyone else, so he could've provided his precious illegal drugs for himself. Anyway!

The fear factor is more than a reality show for the racist; it's also a 'lazy excuse' similar to my friends' way of thinking.

So when a racist finds himself in a position of power over

non-racists, say as a supervisor for example, they may use that position to stifle a non-member's growth, again because they are not one of them.

That's the fake, "taking money out of my pocket" excuse. See, it makes 'cents' to be a racist.

Oh yeah, by the way, my father always said, "money is man-made," so don't be tripping over any green pieces of paper. Ha!!!!

Thanks Father, because of those teachings I never was, nor will I ever be, what one might call money hungry. Somebody should have told my friend.

Anyway!

Within reason, it's okay to aspire to higher heights, financially, for the betterment of you and your family. It depends on your purpose.

What's up with the fantasy, "I just got to be rich?"

A lot of us are already rich, emotionally, spiritually, etc. and may not even realize it. See First Steps.

Oh yeah this is the First Steps chapter. Ha!!!!

My friend also had to be fantasizing also about his self worth.

His delusion of grandeur is common in most criminals. He is of the mentality that would think, "I would never work for that paltry salary," or "that's too far for me to go to work."

Yet criminals want soooo much. But are unwilling to get up everyday and go to work towards that fake happiness.
They'd rather have a slice from that fictitious pie in the sky or steal whatever it is they think they need.

The gold watch, those pearl earrings, the Air Jordan gym shoes, why pay when you can steal. Working is for chumps, take the easy way out, be a racist, get a few slaves, be a plunderer. Get my drift?

You know, a lot of financially rich people would probably be the first ones to tell us that money doesn't buy happiness. The music group The Beatles already told us money can't buy you love.

Then again, tell that to former madam Heidi Fleiss. Ha!!!!

When a racist gets in power, former governor George Wallace for example, they can easily make a lot of people's lives miserable and not be penalized for it, unless you want to count George Wallace being paralyzed.

That was God's will.

Anyway, what kind of deviant mind could concoct the different schemes and plots that would lead to such widespread abnormal criminal behavior?

The same kind of deviant mind as my friends.

Which leads right to my solution for racism: 1. Always strive for higher levels of education. Never allow yourself to be referred to as ignorant and 2. Get registered and vote with intelligence. Don't just vote for a candidate because someone told you to, investigate the individual, and make sure you are not putting a lunatic in public office that'll shout "You Lie" at the President of the United States while he is speaking to the house and the world.

I doubt if you'll find any self-proclaimed racist with a legitimate college degree, if so then find out what their grade point average was. Ha!!!

See, again, I feel strongly that you can't be intelligent AND prejudiced at the same time; you are either one or the other. If a racist does have a high GPA I'll guess they probably cheated their way through school.

OOOOOOOPS, there I go generalizing again, I don't want to discriminate.

Remember there WAS an era when people would go to a lot of trouble to prevent blacks from attending the same schools as white kids, or prevent a black person from voting in ANY elections. The KKK guy's used to really go to a lot of trouble to make sure that wouldn't happen.

Perhaps they still are.

Don't even go there.

Where???

Florida…oooooops.

Anyway, it was really rather simple for me to figure out this solution to counter greed and ignorance.

If the KKK guys don't like it, then I do love it.

Simple, right?

Do the opposite of what the bad guy is promoting.

Don't be a follower, be a leader.

Don't be ignorant, CHOOSE to be educated.

Don't allow people to take away your God-given right as an American citizen to have your voting ability compromised.

Hello Ohio.

I said don't go there.

Sorry…. I forgot.

Anyway, the first step is to love yourself and don't ever put others above you.

Finding true love will be the least of your worries.

Loving yourself is the first step to loving someone. Ha!!!!!

JUST CAN'T LIVE MY LIFE ALONE

No man is an island
No matter where ever I roam…
It's hard, still I can imagine
I will find a place to call my home

Maybe, maybe it's me
Every time I think its love wonder what I was thinking of
One thing that I know
We just can't live our lives alone

We just can't live
Our lives alone
How can that be
A happy home
To only know
Like my own
We just can't live

We just can't live
Our lives alone
Cause man needs friends
So we can grow
Just can't live
Our lives alone
We just can't live

Sometimes it crosses my mind
Why does this have to be?
Something's wrong with everyone else
Cause nothing's wrong with me

Maybe, maybe it's me
Every time I think its love wonder what I was thinking of
There's one thing that I know
We just can't live our lives alone

Chapter 6

New Style.... What's Up?

It's a small world after all. With all the differences that people have, what about our similarities? Everybody goes to the bathroom the same way. We all got to eat. People are basically the same all over the globe.

There is a song made popular by Barbara Streisand that goes something like "People, people who need people, are the luckiest people in the world."

I grew up, if I do say so myself, very popular. I can honestly say that throughout my formative years I was very, very popular. In grammar school, but particularly at Mendel Catholic High School on the far south side of Chicago there I was truly living the life of Riley.

It was then that I won a dance contest on Soul Train, started a dance and social club called "The Doctors," played in the high school marching band, and basically was a school ambassador. I left out some other things but I think you get the point. Ha!!!!

As I grew older, the thousands of friends and associates I had accumulated in high school began to somewhat dwindle away. Consequently I would occasionally bump into old acquaintances while out and about the windy city of Chicago. New friends also came and went on with their lives. Nothing personal, that's just how life goes.

Although, I have been extremely fortunate to still be in touch with people like Warren McBride, Greg Howard and the rest of The Howard family, Atty. Lerone Bennett III his wife Janet, Wayne Williams, Jamie Shelton, Calvin Parks, Grace LaJoy Little and family, Summerville, Jamie Mayes, The Ebony Gents, Pettiford Family, Steve Taylor, Dana Marberry, David Ireland, Principal Richard Smith, Paul Scott, Henry "Don't leave that jacket lying around" Hawkins, Shane Price, Sharon, Cheryll, Mona, Roz, Jo-Jo, April, Carla, Lori, Olive, Laurie, Verlane, Jan, Carmen, Monica Morrow, Syxx Ward, Lester McCarroll, Jon Merrill likes this, Curtis Mayfield III, Sabrina, Frank, Kyle Moon, Hampton and Banks, Earl G., Kaye C., Stan "Goobie" Williams, Tony's Smith-Moton-Johnson-and Summerville, the 1st person to purchase my songbook Ms. Mary Murray also known as the White Panther, my awesome facebook family... The beautiful and talented Ms. Ilyasah Shabazz, Dominique Romain, Angie Hall-Witherspoon, Corrie McCall, Robert "Happy" Walker, Elizabeth Pham, Nicole McGill, Suwana and Sunshine, Kurita, Dawn Glover, Jamie L Payne, Christi Love, SaRah, the artist formerly known as Stephanie Gadlin....;0) Ha!! Gwen Wood, Geri Pettis, Nathan Snodgrass, Anh Vu, James "Truthpaste" Hannah, HOTEP famo, Lisa Rayel Jeffrey, Tricia Harris, Barbara Sanders, Alicia M Mathews (can I get that number?) ;0) Ha!!...and my man Paul Lee...it's just way too many people for me to mention in this songbook..

Yet and still there were some really rough times when we lost touch with each other. It is a belief that people rarely keep the same friends they had in grammar school or high school for the rest of their lives anyway.

I have to admit, there was a void I experienced in my life when I wasn't communicating with my close friends.

There became a need to reach out and reacquaint myself with my "old friends" for self-fulfillment. Emotionally, I guess, I needed people around me, who could share with me and help me with whatever I was celebrating or struggling with.

Are you much different? Ha!!!

When something happens to you, who's the first person you'd call or better yet send a text message? A family member, friend, or perhaps a lover?

Or, do you keep everything locked up inside, a trait many of us are guilty of, me included.

My point is we wouldn't have much of a life if we chose to be alone all the time. If I decided to have no one to talk to, look at, yell at, read about, or no one to play with, as my nephew Matteo says, I might be miserable. What if there was no one to ever eat with at dinnertime, and what if there was no one to marry.

As quiet as it's kept, we just can't prefer to live our lives alone.

Now the racist, on the other hand, is under the delusion that the world was built solely for one purpose, THAT being only to please whatever particular race they are associated with.

To be honest I have no argument with someone's desire to be with his or her own race. It's just that when they start spewing the hatred stuff, it becomes destructively unacceptable, even illegal.

Lets take those Aryans for example, also known as Caucasian gentiles. The Aryan nazis wanted to be alone so bad they started a WAR with what's his name, oh yeah Hitler.

Now go back to my ignorance quotient, nuff said!

We will never know, but, for the sake of speculation, what if the nazis had been successful in ridding the world of everyone they hated? I would venture to guess that with this sort of mentality, after they realized the different race wasn't the ROOT of all their troubles, as first thought, they would find something else to try and exterminate. Some other excuse! Ha!!!!

The sort of mentality that would blindly attempt to eliminate an entire race is absolutely capable of not being satisfied after that race was gone.

Next they would probably blame poor folks for something or anyone who drives an automatic clutch. What about overweight Aryans, they've got to go, or better yet underweight Aryans, or maybe Aryans who can play basketball (oooops that'll never happen...Ha!!! See Dirk Nowitzki, technically an Aryan and all-star member of the Dallas Mavericks basketball team never the less an Aryan guy that CAN hoop.) But do you feel me?

In the documentary I saw about Hitler it told about the time during his rise to political fame he was associated with a group called SSA that was different from the SS.

Well Hitler was gaining ground as far as becoming a recognizable public figure in Germany early in his career and apparently a deal was struck for him to get to that next level of leadership.

The deal was he had to kill all his SSA buddies and recognize the SS only. No problem.

Just like that, the SSA members were killed. Ha!!!

Did you ever know somebody who was just never satisfied?

No matter what you would do to try to make them happy, they still weren't happy. Don't those kind of people just get on your last nerves? Those darned nazis!!

Ooooooops there I go discriminating. I got to be careful folks; I do not want to fall into that trap.

There is another racist group I saw a documentary on about a group calling themselves skinheads.

They struck me as very interesting. I came away viewing them as young, desperate, and lonely individuals who resorted to this gang because perhaps they felt abandoned, by their families or by society. They'd been "kicked to the curb" and fortunately they had bumped into an elder skinhead waiting with arms wide open.

This devil…I mean elder ended up in jail but even without his leadership the followers and members struck me as being extremely confused.

I wonder if death is a badge of courage for these Hitler-like worshippers? There was the same old complaint about minorities taking jobs away from them, at the same time I'm thinking, "You're not the most hygienic-looking people." I'm sure that had nothing to do with your being unemployed.

Heck I know I've just had all kinds of jobs just fall out of the sky into my lap with no skills or intelligence quotient necessary. Simply being black has made my life so wonderful in America. Ha!!!!

Yeah right, anyway.

I also noticed the skinheads constantly refer to themselves as a gang, which to me is an acknowledgement that they are not productive members of society.

I mean why keep complaining that the government allows crack houses to exist but keep trying to shut down the skinheads. Duhhhhhhh.

In other words BOTH OF YOU ARE BAD!!!! Get it! If the only comparison YOU can come up with are drug-dealing gangs and crack houses, as opposed to the Boy Scouts or schools, then perhaps you need to stop fooling yourselves.

It's easy to innocently discriminate.

Have you ever been in or out of a clique, social club, fraternity or sorority?

The truth is we may have discriminated against someone already and not even realized it. Shame on us.

The proverbial pot calling the kettle black, or African-American.

Again I want to say that I truly couldn't find much wrong with the skinheads' argument about wanting to be alone so badly, away from the maddening "other-heads."

It's when you start rallying your buddies to wreck havoc

on the community because your leader got locked up for BREAKING THE LAW is when I have a problem!!! Duhhhh.

Hey I have an idea! Why not leave America. I'm sure there is a filthy, unsanitary island someplace where you can get a job uncontested simply because you want to hate people. Good luck…Ha!!!

I even remember, to my dismay, watching Real Sports w/ Bryant Gumble talk about how in Europe during soccer games, there's an entire section in the bleachers dedicated to Hitler worship and antagonizing black players every time one takes the field with bananas AND insults hurled at them.

There has to be plenty of options for you outside of the good ole USA. Stop letting America hold you back. I only hope when you get there you are with the SS or is it the SSA or maybe the XYZ, oh well good luck, you're definitely going to need it in case they suddenly develop a change of heart.

Anyway, remember Dave from the racism workshop on the Oprah show? He was confused, remember? Well join the club. We aren't perfect, nobody is, not even the Aryans. Ha!!!!

So don't feel too guilty if you look back at situations you were directly involved in that could be categorized as prejudicial and realize things could have been handled differently.

Just apologize.

Do what YOU can to right any wrongs and try not to ever let it happen again. And oh yeah, to all you racists out there brave enough to get this far in my book, knock it off.

Quit tripping.

There are more ways to make the world a wonderful place other than chastising a certain group of people simply for being different. Nobody likes a bully and the Lord doesn't like ugly! Ha!!!!

You know, growing up in my community, as a whole, people there would tend to stay within the immediate vicinity of the neighborhood. It was considered a big deal to go a couple miles to downtown Chicago. People might believe that it was soooo far away.

This could result in a person having a closed mind as well.

Please, be brave enough to venture outside of your respective neighborhoods. There's a great big old world out there WAITING FOR YOU to take part.

Chicago is a great place to meet various cultures. You got your Asian, Italian, Polish, Irish, Black, Croatian and Hispanic communities and more to grow your mind.

You remember how I discovered that Native Americans prefer to be recognized by their tribes? I wonder why they feel that way?

Well there's one way to find out and that is by asking one of them. That opportunity will never occur if we stay within the borders of our neighborhoods or closed mindsets.

Venture out, see the world, feel the grass between your toes, take a ride on a boat or better yet go horseback riding, live life to the fullest. It has been said, "you can watch the game in the stands or get out on the field and be a player."

Either way make sure you know the rules of the game.

There's one thing that I know, we just can't live our lives alone. Ha!!!

VOTE

Keenan:
People get ready
It's your time
To vote

People get ready it's your time

Bahb:
Look at what we're facing   (Look at it)
All across the nation   (How 'bout it?)
High rising inflation   (Awww yeah)
Big time discrimination

The lacking education   (Look at it)
We need to choose an administration   (How 'bout it?)
Can you dig my conversation   (Awww yeah)
Get registered and VOTE!!!!

Keenan:
Every girl
Every man
Time to take a stand

Family and Friends
Got to make a demand

Vote because you have to
Stop letting them laugh at you
Ain't proper if you think you

Can take it as a joke

Chapter 7

What's Up "Yes We Can" Brand New Style Players...Ha!!!

Well, I must say I am more than surprised that from the beginning of this tiny songbook, to this chapter, we were able to get Senator Barack Obama elected President of the United States. Wow that was fast...Ha!!!

Actually I began writing this tiny songbook about the year 2002 and at that time there was NO WAY I would have imagined the USA finally getting a President that can hoop.

Weird that this very same subject came up at that Oprah Winfrey workshop and no one had a clue...I'm sure the closest person we could've come up with at the time was General Colin Powell as a potential winner but I'm not so sure he can hoop though...Ha!!!

All you young people out there that are reading this can only imagine how your grandparents and great grandparents and their elders must feel, them knowing that the right for 'us' to vote is a recent American gesture that was never supposed to result in an outcome like what has recently changed history.

Now all you hear is how anyone can be the president and it doesn't matter anymore what you are or where you came from… all I could say is you're right.

If George W. Bush can be president…anyone can become the President…. Double Ha!!!!

People have the audacity to say that same thing about recent Supreme Court Justice Sotomayor as if she/he wasn't really qualified for their respective ascension.

There goes that superman syndrome again…'any black dude can go to Harvard and be a Senator'…what's so difficult about that???

Those are the only people I hang out with, Black United States Senators that graduated from Harvard. They're a dime a dozen. Ha!!!

It was a long campaign though wasn't it? First it was Hillary Clinton and John Edwards and then it was John McCain and Sarah Palin and throughout every victorious step closer I STILL never gave Obama a chance of winning.

That's right, still jaded even after the election results in November 2008 came back I still didn't believe it…in the back of my mind I was thinking THEY can still come up with something, they did it before.

Wait a minute…don't go there.

Oh all right…but it isn't like there was only one person booing "dubya" when he finally left office.

Anyway what about when Senator Obama was being sworn in and the judge made a mistake with the oath? I was like this is how they're gonna get him…Ha!!!

It almost worked but the Black Senator from Harvard apparently was ready for that blindside attack also and recited back the correct words to the judge and was sworn in again later just to cover his bases.

Then and only then did I feel comfortable calling the Black Senator from Harvard 'President Barack Obama.' It's weird but apparently a lot of journalist and media people still have trouble calling him President also, even to this day, almost 1 later but I won't go there…Haters.

Hey!!! No whining remember.

I am writing this chapter September 2009 and wow, has it been something seeing a campaign and election that wasn't supposed to be about race BE about race so much that I believe we are finally becoming numb to the mention of the subject.

There was even a daily program during the campaign called "Race for The White House."

Sure you have your Rush's and this new kid Glen something constantly fanning the flame for their minions but when politicians try to jump on the bandwagon of nonsense they are finally finding themselves looking ridiculous.

I'm sure some republicans out there reading this songbook want to shout "YOU LIE" at me right now but hey, I'm not the President of the United States. Besides if you were to have your way with me I'm going to "DIE QUICKLY" anyhow so please don't interrupt, that's rude.

This songbook has been a long arduous campaign as well, when I review it I have to smile when I go back over the things that I wrote about and what has transpired since then.

For example we are still in Wars overseas, the 2016 Olympics will be in Rio, I have become addicted to something called face book and Ron Artest the "Tru Warrior" is playing with the Los Angeles Lakers this upcoming season, I'm sure in a quest for a championship alongside, that's right Kobe Bryant. Good luck guys, unless you're playing my boys Derrick Rose, Kirk Hinrich and The Chicago Bulls for the Championship.

This is wild because when I started this book Derrick Rose was still in H.S. in Chicago at legendary Simeon H.S. home of player Nick Anderson, coach Bob Hambric RIP and player Benjamin Wilson RIP killed in his prime near his school.

Wow from Dantrell Davis to Benjamin Wilson to Darrion Albert (Fenger H.S. student beaten to death.) Chicago has a lot of history to cry about. I already talked about how happy the kkk is that we black folk are eagerly killing each other.

These young black kids today don't have a clue about where they came from or where they are headed.

But if you want to know about a stripper pole, the club or some Patron liquor they will more than likely be able to give you a novels worth of facts about that plain and simply because we little black folk are LAZY.

It's presumed easier to follow in the footsteps of laziness than the footsteps of some hard workers. But I'm gonna let you in on a little secret…it's all hard work.

Yep, it's even hard work to be LAZY. In the long run you will still have to figure out how will my laziness help me survive, just like a hard worker has to calculate how their hard work will pay off.

So guess what…you're only delaying the obvious. Ain't nothing new!!

I know you young black folk want to believe and you probably want the rest of the world to believe that lazy grammar and wearing your pants around your knees is normal until you get ready to apply for a job and you never get any positive results… it will become obvious. Ha!!!

How about that black kid acting/talking 'white' over there going to work with his pants fastened and above average vocabulary…it will become obvious.

Last but not least there's a person of color in the White House that can hoop who you can use for inspiration…it should start becoming obvious right aboooouuuut NOW.

Ha!!!

To some people out there it might still be somewhat cloudy so I want to have an election.

That's right people get ready to vote or should I say choose because that is basically what an election is…choosing right? It always comes back around to choice…. Ha!!!

I'm running against the racist, the racist mentality and the racist ideology. I want the racist to lose.

When the racist makes a remark that the world can hear I want to be there in his face to remind them how ridiculous they are.

Are you with me?

Remember that racist record company? I want these songs to become like nursery rhymes and people able to sing/recite them when faced with nonsense.

In other words when a kid tells us he's thinking about dropping out of school to join a gang is he/she reaching for the "ceiling or the floor?" That line is from "Gonna Be A Better Day." Ha!!

Are you with me? I need your votes!!!!

My fellow non-racist Americans I come before you today and everyday humbled by your acknowledgement but I am asking for more out of you…I need you to reach out and touch somebody's hand to make this world a better place…YES WE CAN!!!!

Are you with me? I need your votes!!!!

It's got to stop sooner or later and I think it would be wonderful to see in my lifetime the tide starting to turn with our young people refusing to settle for mediocrity.

I don't care if you're parents are there, half there, absent, abusive, alcoholics or even incarcerated, all of that is an excuse to hold you back and keep you down…. go find somebody to help you…I'm on face book…Ha!!!

That's my goal to build a foundation to be able to impact people's lives.

Are you with me? I NEED YOUR VOTES!!!!

You have already done more than enough getting this songbook but the goal is to make the racists feel beat down and never want to get back up, so tell all your friends that you are fed up and you are not going to take it anymore.

We can do this. Yes We Can!!!

Are you with me?

People get ready…it's your time…. Ha!!!

LIES

THIS IS DEDICATED TO DERRION ALBERT AND LOUIS BUCKNER VICTIMS OF CHICAGO VIOLENCE. RIP

Easily we are deceived
Sometimes I can't believe
It hurts me emotionally why can't we live like brothers

I wanna throw up both my hands
But I'm not God I'm just a man
Trying to make you understand how much we need each other
We don't need the lies

Everyday I get in my ride when I need to go outside
Can't drive if I close my eyes but I want to badly

See it's just too big to hide
Whatever happened to the pride?
Still another brother dies never knowing what he could've had
We don't need the lies

Now if you're sick and tired of all the lies
Better open up your ears and open up your eyes
Stop being blind and use your mind
Cause in due time you will be fine

Lies upon lies upon lies...the pain hurts me so deep inside
Lies upon lies upon lies...keeps bringing tears to my eyes

It surprises me how wealth
Can put your pride upon a shelf
I wanna pinch myself to make sure that I'm not dreaming
I'm really getting scared cause it seems like no one cares
This might be a nightmare...nothings there but screaming and the lies!!!!

Chapter 8

Hey New Style

Remember when I was talking about ignorance and greed being the origins of racism?

These traits can also work to the benefit of the racist in a different way.

What about when the abused or unaware race CHOOSES ignorance and greed, then guess what, they are assisting the racist's movement. Ha!!!!

Say what?

That's right, you begin to blindly help the KKK guys.

We black folk should be ashamed of ourselves!!!!

Have you ever heard of a guy named Martin Luther King Jr.????

I coined a phrase a long time ago, "The Black Man is the klu klux klan!"

What does that mean?

Well when we black dudes continue to do negative things voluntarily, who needs the KKK to hold us back. Young black folk are innocently holding us back?

Allow me to elaborate.

Take the so-called 'gang-banger,' a struggling young black person out here trying to sell illegal dope because he has been easily deceived into giving up on trying to get an education. By the way that mentality is for losers.

Think about it.

Struggling young black people today are easily led to believe the 'easy money' is in peddling drugs to the community.

You're either part of the solution or you're a part of the problem.

Perhaps I should note that the struggling black folk are not the only ones dealing drugs, other communities do struggle with illegal drugs as well, I am however unfamiliar with them so for the sake of this story, I will stay focused on black folk.

Now, don't get me wrong, if a person wants to get high they're going to always find a way to get high with or without a drug dealer's assistance, believe me, I know.

But let me finish.

So, the struggling young black person decides to join a gang. Forget respecting your parents (if you have any) or teacher. As a matter of fact just stop going to school all together, because they believe it is going to 'benefit' them.

Don't forget about all the ladies the guys are going to have as girlfriends, with the bling bling.

Oh yeah, this can lead to that other big problem, teenaged single parent pregnancies gone rampant, but that's another book. Anyway.

Struggling young black people apparently are ready and willing to settle for looking over their shoulders as a career, until one day here comes a police officer tapping on that same shoulder with the handcuffs ready.

Now the struggling young black person is off to jail, a "vacation" that you were planning all along unconsciously anyway; it was just a matter of time.

Note: About now is when you are supposed to begin to realize that you have been victimized. Anyway.

You go to jail and get entrenched even more in that negative gang mentality lifestyle because now it has really, truly, become a matter of survival to know what a freaking cigarette is worth.

When you were out in the free world, life, as it always was, turned out to also be a matter of survival. But the struggling young black person took the supposedly easy way out by attempting to SELL illegal drugs as a career move.

For some strange reason a lot of people have come to the conclusion that going to school or work every day is for suckers.

I'm here to tell you that this is a LIE. That's why I wrote this songbook. I'm begging and I'm pleading!!

There's nothing stronger than a person who gets up and goes to a true legal job every day to take care of his business and family.

Try it and see if it is easy. No it's not easy, but neither is jail... Ha!!!

To a confused, young black wanna-be drug-dealer convict, living a life along the straight and narrow just didn't seem logical before, until, compared to now when he's looking out from behind bars.

Emotionally, it hurts me that all races, creeds, and colors can't live together like true brothers and sisters to promote positivism for each other.

We don't need the lies.

"How do drugs get over here in the first place?" "I'm not the problem I'm just a provider." These are nothing but excuses also known as LIES.

Stop allowing our children to believe this nonsense. Ha!!!!

Anyway, perhaps the young black people will eventually get out of jail, then what options are left?

Where are they going to work, who is going to trust and help them?

Of course, "the old gang."

You'll TRY to stay out of trouble, but the old crowd will want to celebrate your freedom. Next thing you know, you're doing the same things you were doing before.

LYING.

All the while the KKK is sitting back on the sidelines drinking lemonade. They don't have to do anything because the good young black people are doing everything for them.

We're dropping out of school way too readily. (One of my remedies for this illness.)

There goes the higher education endeavor.

Election, what election?? (One of my other remedies.)

If it had not been for Barack Obama running for President of the United States there probably would've been no youthful enthusiasm and now after he was elected they've reverted back to the overall negativity instead of maintaining the positive momentum.

You get the drift?

I hate to stereotype, but I just don't see lazy gangs suddenly having spirited debates about any political issues or aspirations, sorry.

I believe anything can happen. Keep the faith brothers and sisters. Ha!!!

I just realized that perhaps the reason some black ex-convicts angle toward the music industry or Hollywood as an answer is because the special rewards appear so much like what was being chased in the first place.

Although that special celebrity status and the financial rewards, I'm sure, may be the hardest work of all to attain.

Just ask Jay-Z or Beyonce how easy it was for them.

This is also perhaps why so much fan support is based in the struggling communities because somebody special finally made it 'out.'

Anyway.

Did I mention the black on black crime?

Why should the KKK guys lynch a brother when we'll probably

wipe each other out anyway shooting up our playgrounds and killing innocent youth 'by accident?'

Long live Dantrell Davis; a Chicago youth killed by accident in a housing project to Derrion Albert the Chicago Fenger H.S. student who was beaten to death in a riot.

We should be ashamed of ourselves.

Ever heard of a dude named Dr. Martin Luther King Jr.?

I'm sure he'd be very proud of how easily we struggling black folk have sold out.

We black folk are supposed to be strong, not weak illegal drug-dealers.

If you STRUGGLING YOUNG BLACK PEOPLE believe it is stronger to sell drugs or it's stronger to drop out of school, then I'm here to tell you that this is a LIE.

It surprises me how wealth can put our pride up on a shelf. Sometimes I want to pinch myself to make sure that I'm not dreaming.

See I'm really getting scared.

Cause it seems like no one cares.

This might be a nightmare.

Nothing's there, but screaming and the LIES. Ha!!!!

Remember when my union steward from the phone company was arguing against affirmative action basically because he believed struggling black folk should be able to pull themselves up by their own bootstraps?

That was a heck of a compliment. His feelings are widespread. I happen to share those same beliefs.

I call it the SUPERMAN stigma. Ha!!!

What is really being said is that black people are really awesome or special when they want to be.

The expectations are high and well they should be.

I personally hold us to an extremely high standard based on my different interactions throughout my lifetime.

I have witnessed some remarkably talented individuals who

would have gone unnoticed if I hadn't bothered to dig a little deeper and gotten to actually know some struggling black folk.

Far too many times we will settle for mediocrity when above average or excellence is right around the bend.

This to me is the curse of the Black American. Ha!!!!

Not to mention the "confusion" of striving for what we THINK is sooo important, also known as "Keeping up with the Joneses."

What an imbalance.

On one hand we are comfortable with mediocrity and on the other hand we find ourselves chasing after some materialistic "golden idol" nonsense.

When will we ever figure out the right way to go?

Can't explain what we're asked to know. Ha!!!

Well, a lot of us have come to the conclusion that knowledge is 'King,' as in Martin Luther.

Jump on the bandwagon. Not lackadaisically, but with the ferociousness of a Vince Carter slam-dunk.

You'll be surprised at how previously closed doors will open up to you, and the simple mysteries of the world will start to become a lot clearer when we strive for higher levels of education.

Struggling Young Black Person, gang-banger wanna be, YOU ARE GREAT when you want to be. This attribute also makes it too easy to be sub-par we only put a little effort towards that sub-par-wanna-be-gang-banger reality.

Remember, the devil is lonely ya'll.

Movie director Spike Lee said it best, "Do the Right Thing!" Ha!!!

And oh yeah…stop recruiting our black youth for this negative activity, the fake career in illegal drug sales.

What kind of future can you promise them?

Are you being honest with them?

The KKK would be proud of you recruiting young people for crime, guaranteeing the devastation and destruction of one more 'worthless life.'

Am I coming through?

I hope so. Ha!!!

Stop being victimized into believing this is 'your' street corner and if somebody doesn't move there's going to be bloodshed.

This is part of the basis why I wish the government would legalize drugs, so we can stop killing each other over this nonsense.

President Barack Obama, pretty please with brown sugar on top legalize it.

Let's sell crack at Walgreen's for God's sake.

The drug addicts and sellers will get the stuff anyway.

Let the police worry about something else for a change, other than Lil Ace on the block selling dime bags.

Oh, that's right, now some "kid" is supposed to be America's most wanted criminal all of a sudden!

I don't think so.

What about all these terrorists, we can focus our attention on them better and with more resources. Ha!!!

Remember, if a person wants to get high they are going to get high!!!

I know to some of you this may sound insane, but drastic measures call for drastic steps to be taken.

Look on the bright side. If drugs were legalized, the government will make a ton of money. And our communities can stop fearing the killing of another innocent over this 'junk,' never knowing what they could've had.

Perhaps the price of gasoline will also magically lower. Ha!!!!

Anyway.

Remember, these illegal drug-dealers and such are not rocket scientists.

Remember, they more than likely have dropped out of school, so when they conclude that the easiest solution to their problem is to kill someone; they don't take time to go to a shooting range for practice; they just start shooting.

I am not going to lie.

Unfortunately for me, I have gotten high before and I was way too well acquainted with the sort of fellows I am now criticizing.

This is also why I feel justified making these statements, because I saw what I'd call the 'confusion' in their eyes and their lives.

Believe it or not they may not feel they are doing anything wrong. They may even be under the delusion that this is some sort of a noble gesture selling illegal drugs.

But it never failed, that ultimately one day, I would always see in their eyes the hope for that elusive, fantastical 'big score' so they can stop selling this negative stuff to people and perhaps lead a normal, legal life.

That can also be referred to as a 'dream.'

The hope to one day lead a normal lifestyle, without having to look over your shoulder all the time to see if the police are watching you.

A natural goal, to lead a 'normal life' without having to worry about your family's safety and well being after the elusive "big score."

We don't need the LIES. Ha!!

It has nothing to do with, "how it gets here"…books are here and I don't see you pushing libraries.

C'mon Mr. President who cares what people think…it's long overdue.

So confused young black kid, if you're out there reading this, and you want to sell drugs to our people as a lazy means to get rich, then just go to school and become a freaking pharmacist. Ha!!!!

Stop the madness!!

I heard a while back this nazi group held a rally in Ohio that set off a riot because the so-called gang-bangers of the community were so insulted, they retaliated with rocks etc. and the police had to intervene blah blah blah.

I found this very interesting that we struggling black folk know that the nazi mentality is evil and yet the gang-banger-wanna-be's throwing rocks are unconsciously assisting the KKK in the destruction of the black community.

Some might call that being hypocritical. Double Ha!!!!

I want to throw up both my hands and make it all go away, but I'm not God. I'm just a man, so I wrote this songbook in hopes that you struggling young black people will understand.

I am extremely sensitive to your plight but a change has got to come.

You have way more power than you realize.

Help end racism, stop "helping" the KKK guys.

Please Mr. President.

We don't need the lies!!! Ha!!!

True story of Papa Dallas...A little girl who was sitting on her grandfather's lap in the early 1930's asked why he could not see and what were the scars around his eyes. He responded that as a boy he would sneak away under a tree to learn to read. When the overseer saw him he was beaten to within an inch of his life and then his eyes were gouged out with a hot iron in front of all of the rest of the slaves on the plantation as an example of what would happen if they tried to learn to read. The little girl began to cry. Papa Dallas responded, "Don't cry baby girl; but learn as much as YOU can, read as much as YOU can, and go as high as YOUR education will take YOU. He paused and said, "and tell everyone my story." (Franklin, R 2003) Thanks Ural H. Hill Ph.D.,L.P.C.

Assistant Professor
Texas Southern University
College of Education
Ha!!!!

WARS

Soldier
Wake up in the morning to the reveille
About a half a million places that I'd rather be
When I open my eyes what do I see?
Death and destruction all around me
I'm caught up in the middle I don't understand
Is the world a better place cause you kill another man?
It's ok over here cause I'm in another land!
Even though I got a gun I'd rather shake your hand.

Civilian
I wake up every morning and this is what I see
Yellow tape surrounding the buildings next to me
There's a war going on like Desert Storm
But this one's on the street in front of my home
Cars being shot up, brothers getting locked up
A bad situation I'm too close to get caught up
Bodies on the street man everywhere
Babies won't come out cause they're too scared
Black on black crime I sho ain't lying
Every ten seconds there's a person dying
Too hard to keep being but I keep seeing
Bodies being dropped by the dozens kid
I strive...cause I got to stay alive
In the middle of a war you got to pray to survive

Soldier
Too late now I got you in my sight
Gently squeeze the trigger better hold on tight
Me and my boys coming for you in the middle of the night
Both sides believe that they are right
Click BOOM another brother's gone
Been a long long time since sticks and stones
Be glad when it's over hope I can go home
To fight another war keeping up with the Jones

Civilian
A mothers only born on the street warring
But ain't no love for him cause his daddy's gone away from here
Confronted by his peers
Either join in or you'll disappear
Left with no choice he accepts the deal
Not knowing the danger that lies here
Now he's out on the corner with a baseball cap
Cocked to the right with the tek in sight
A gang war but the other's never told him
Don't get caught on the corner after dark
A car pulls up somebody yells "DUCK"
Too late he's already been stuck
For tempting his luck
Man it's too rough
Lost at birth but you know what's worse
A mother sends her only born away in a hearse

Gone before she got to know him
Didn't get a chance to hold him
The world is getting colder
The killings getting bolder
How many times have I told cha?
You're not getting any older
Start thinking like a soldier
Remember what I told cha

Wars over here Wars over there
It's about time that we get scared
Stop pretending nobody cares
Unless you got people over there

Better shout about it if you dare
No casualties is something rare
(That's) Why NSP's everywhere
Open your ears and you will hear

"The Kingdom of the Lion" by Aesop

"The beasts of the field and forest had a Lion as their king. He was neither wrathful, cruel nor tyrannical, but just and gentle as a king could be. During his reign he made a royal proclamation for a general assembly of all the birds and beasts, and drew up conditions for a universal league, in which the Wolf and the Lamb, the Panther and the Kid, the Tiger and the Stag, the Dog and the Hare, should live together in perfect peace and amity. The Hare said, "Oh, how I have longed to see this day, in which the weak shall take their place with impunity by the side of the strong." And after the Hare said this, he ran for his life."

Chapter 9

What's up New Style???

This is a very special chapter because I am writing it in September of 2007 opposed to some of the rest of the chapters that originated in and around 2002. Although I have been diligent in my heart to complete this task before me of writing a book, or should I say "songbook" about trying to end racism, the obstacles I have had to face along the way were very daunting to say the least.

However, I'm still here, alive and well and as you can see I didn't allow anything to stop me from completing the first 'real' major task of my life that 'you know who' chose for me. Ha!!!!

Perhaps that is the moral of this chapter, keeping the faith and never giving up hope no matter what problems occur because it's gonna be a better day.

Believers know we're only passengers anyway because 'you know who' is driving, that's why I chose to sit back and enjoy the ride a long time ago.

I really want this chapter to try and figure out why is everything sooo hard? For example, trying to get people to see the logical answers only to be confronted with some utter nonsense in response.

Are we that jaded or is it always going to be a tug of war when important decisions have to be made?

The Aesop fable at the top of the chapter was chosen for its insightfulness.

This guy Aesop was an awesome storyteller who incorporated animals in most of his stories to help get his point across.

I'm sure most of the people reading this are familiar with another of his works, "The Tortoise and the Hare" and how "slow but steady" will win the race. Ha!!!

Wow, that theme even applies to my plight attempting to finish this book. Perhaps I will need to allude to that later.

Anyway!!!

That Aesop was a bad dude!!!! He definitely was way ahead of his time. When you readers have some free time look him up at your local library, just tell them Fireman Bahb sent you.

The reason I wanted that fable to kick off this chapter is because it is indicative of a lot of our attitudes as human beings. Sure everyone can wish for things to change for the better but history tells some of you not to get your hopes up.

History tells us to "run for our lives" like the character in the fable because it's "no use" things will never get better.

We may as well assimilate to popular behavior.

Run for your life, run for your gun or run to illegal drugs is a lot of the attitudes that overtake people when we should instead run to school, run to our families rescue or, most importantly, run to 'you know who.'

It's a war going on like Desert Storm but this one's on the street in front of my home!!! Ha!!!!

The war between believers and naysayers is a never-ending saga. The battle has been going on for soo long that a lot of people would rather try to keep up with the Jones' rather than be original.

Ideas like wearing your pants around your thighs originated in jails and to me have seen their hey day. I am tired of seeing peoples' underwear, especially when it's dirty. Get yours pants off the ground!!!.

Ha!!!!!

It's time to come up for air and breath in the opportunities for individuality that "you know who" has put in all our hearts and minds to discover, explore and share with the rest of the world. Time to get rid of that defeatist mentality and push ourselves to the limit.

I know it is a lot easier said than done which is exactly why I am declaring war on ineptitude. Ha!!!!!

I have really tried to stay away from the subject of how sorry we black people are becoming but, as of late, I feel extraordinarily compelled to say and do something drastic to stop these bad behaviors before things get worse. Not that there is much more that can go wrong for us!

Don't get me wrong I love my black brothers and sisters but I'm getting me a white girl!!!

Seriously though people that was said in jest but let's be honest, black folk can be scary sometimes. As the music group Public Enemy's member Chuck D once said, "I'm tired of smart people ACTING dumb!"

In other words, history has proven that black people can be many things. We can be strong, handsome, prosperous, resourceful, talented, creative, generous, logical, conscientious, well mannered, loving creatures.

Oh yeah I almost forgot, athletic. It seems you can't talk about black people unless you reference their athleticism.

Wait a minute!! Don't go there. You already talked about that!!!

Ohhh...all right.

Anyway, getting back to what I was saying, remember no one

is perfect, so for all our good traits we can also be seen as weak, ugly, crooked, treacherous, lazy, greedy, illogical, selfish, rude and jealous people.

The problem is I feel like we are settling more for the latter traits then the aforementioned ones and that is a gourmet chef's recipe for disaster. Ha!!!!

I said it before that MLK has got to be turning over in his grave, unable to rest easy because of our blatant disrespect for all that he laid his life on the line for.

We should be ASHAMED of ourselves to pretend it's okay to solicit so much profanity in movies, comedy and music only to later attempt to excuse it as our nature and environment that created this acceptable monster.

No time like the present to make a change I always say.

To all the so-called artists out there it's time for some real creativity. Stop being lazy and perpetuating the myth that profanity is our acceptable artistic expression.

More and more I am hearing uncomfortable words on network television and radio stations of all places. When New York radio shock jock Don Imus says "nappy headed hoes" are we more upset about the "nappy headed" part of the statement or the "hoes" part of the statement?

Personally I think there is nothing, I repeat absolutely nothing, wrong with being nappy headed.

When Oprah Winfrey had a discussion about this incident on a different show her friend Gail traveled to Spellman, a well-respected university in Atlanta, Georgia that has a black female population, to get their opinions.

It was no surprise to me that the prestigious students at Spellman University were appalled.

I wonder what if Gail had gone to, lets say, the west side of Chicago for example, and gathered thoughts from some of the sister girls hanging out with some home boys wearing the droopy pants. Ha!!!

I venture to guess that their reaction would have been more comical versus outrage and objection.

This attitude is becoming a better depiction of how more and more young black people ONLY strive for mediocrity.

In other words, how dare black folk crave respect?

What did we ever do to earn respect from strangers? If you ain't got no mag rims, let alone a car to dress up with those stupid mags yawl sing about so much.

We don't deserve respect. Ha!!!

If you ain't got no flashy jewelry to wear to an event where your life is endangered. You ain't got's to get no education. You ain't got's to pay for things when you can steal something and try to re-sell it, so who needs a regular job punching a clock. You're smarter than that, you're a hustler N-word, remember. Ha!!!!!

I would laugh if this mentality weren't so sadly widespread. If you don't believe me check the statistics about black males dropping out of school for the street life of selling drugs and all the up and coming wanna be pregnant strippers for example.

I am sure there are plenty of guys in jail for illegal non-violent drug convictions who will readily say they wish they would have stayed in school or sought real employment elsewhere.

What up fool??? Ha!!!!

If you're starting to feel insulted good. It's about time.

Maybe black people will stop settling and "man up" to claim the respect and adoration that is rightfully ours handed down from 'YOU KNOW WHO.'

But wait a minute, don't get happy. We ain't that special.

It's just that we are nowhere near as bad as a lot of black people have come to accept the belief of how bad off black people are destined to be.

All people are special because we are all a gift from 'you know who.' But why is it in America every other race can effortlessly unite for a cause while black people have to behave like crabs in a barrel. Constantly pulling each other down so one can climb on top of each other to reach the so-called top of a barrel?

To the untrained eye it may sound like I am promoting racism, an "us against them" posture.

On the contrary, I just want us to represent 'you know who' the way we are supposed to.

For starters how about learning to speak the English language properly on purpose and not by accident.

For example if you used to "like someone" then you liked them (one syllable) you never like-TED (two syllables) anybody because that's not a word.

You feel me? Ha!!!

Getting back to our reluctance to unite, I want to talk about this illegal immigration issue for a second. The people mainly concerned about the ramifications of new laws etc. are by definition not true American citizens. Yet when faced with an obstacle that affects their "community" negatively said illegal will rally round a flag, UNITED, to voice their opinion, and show their STRENGTH through numbers.

I understand there may be a bit of resentment against illegal immigrants but my point is about their strong showing of unity that can't be denied.

Trying to get black people to unite as a whole is like trying to get a round peg into a square hole, sad to say it appears it just doesn't WANT to happen.

Again, we are up against a defeatist mentality most times BEFORE a movement can even gain any ground.

That's why I wanted to write this songbook, to kick-start a movement toward raising self-esteem and expectations.

I must say when we do come together we are a formidable group because historically our bond is strong.

By that I mean our awareness and adaptability to struggles are well documented.

Yes we can…Ha!!!

Which, again, perplexes me why we don't do better for ourselves because of the raw deal that black people have been dealt historically and today.

I am gonna go back to my mention of black folk taking pride in being an American-American first and a little later we can get cognizant of our African heritage.

Lets take care and focus on the business at hand of educating American people how to sustain forward movement like my former generations did for me.

One step at a time. Ha!!!!!

I never dreamed of embarrassing my family, or race, in public by shouting obscenities on public transportation or around strangers.

I grew to believe to have way more respect for myself than to just brandish about rude and obscene behavior.

Let's do away with dignified people being accused of acting "like a white person."

I'm tired of there only being one smart guy in the clique, how about everyone joining in on the discussion.

Wait a minute, here come the nay Sayers.

Oh that will never happen, we may as well give up.

Well, NO, YOU can give up, but my friends and I have got something else in mind so YOU can stay up in the bleachers.

My friends and me are going to prepare to take the field and get into the game, with the hope of success.

After all we are athletic. Ha!!!!

OOOPs don't go there I said

Sorry, I can't help it.

Yeah as black people we need to stop allowing other people, black or whatever, the ability to dictate our lives and take control of our future and the futures of our children starting right now.

It may sound simple but tomorrow go MAKE SURE that you are registered to vote and use your power intelligently.

That's right I said power. Believe it or not we are powerful contrary to popular belief. Ha!!!

111

A friend of mine once told me, "Why should I vote? It's only a choice between the lesser of two evils."

To me, that is precisely the reason to get out the vote.

If our ONLY choice is two evils then I definitely want the lesser evil one in office.

I also hear friends say how the elections are fixed anyway like what happened in 2000 with Al Gore and Bush in Florida so why bother.

Hold on for a second. Look man, I told you we ain't going there now stop doing that.

Yeah but it's not like I'm the only guy talking about it.

I don't care; we ain't here for that now, so stop it okay?

All right, all right, I promise I won't talk about stuff like that anymore in this chapter.

Are we good?? Are you sure??? Man I'm trying to…Humph

Anyway, as I was saying before I was so rudely interrupted by my conscience, there is this silly notion that the efforts of a few won't make much difference and I'm here to tell you THAT is pure nonsense. Ha!!!!

If I felt that way I wouldn't be speaking to you right now visually or musically. Double Ha!!

Now don't get me wrong you shouldn't have to be celebrated to make a difference.

This songbook, case in point, was considered a waste of time by a lot of people but through some due diligence it can ultimately have the desired impact on society that it deserves.

Strive for higher levels of education; be it formal or otherwise, because applied knowledge is 'Martin Luther' king. Ha!!!

How many times have we gotten a project that required

assembling and attempted to put it together free hand only to finally pull out the instructions and achieve success.

There's a method to this madness that we call life and it's not a secret kept in any closet either.

Although I "can't explain" what we're asked to know it's not like it's Chinese calculus or anything either.

One thing about knowledge gained is how we choose to respond to information received.

Why is it sometimes easy to receive information and other times it is a tug of war?

Perhaps, it is when faced with change we tense up, because our beliefs have gotten us this far and any more new information is like taking on a football team for some people, especially senior citizens.

I remember when my sister and I were managing our traveling modeling troupe in Chicago and one day after a successful fashion show everyone was feeling so proud about the show we just performed that we wanted to celebrate.

Our modeling troupe was like heaven, with all different types of people working together in what had culminated into a family-like atmosphere. Everyone became friends and we really cared for each other.

Anyway, one of the female models suggested we go to Rush Street in Chicago to celebrate because of the great nightlife and I became rather nervous at the suggestion because I knew an ugly monster was about to rear it's ugly head.

You see the girl that suggested Rush Street was white and unbeknownst to her Rush Street has a well-known reputation, in black male circles, of not allowing black guys into their clubs.

It suddenly became aware to me the subject of race had never come up before throughout our modeling companies entire 1-2 year existence.

Pretty remarkable considering the wide mix of people that was in our troupe.

Anyway I tried to politely come up with different suggestions of different places to go and celebrate but Rush Street was the obvious choice because of its central location for everyone.

When it became clear we were going to Rush Street I was compelled to explain to everyone that every time I tried to go there I wasn't able to go inside of those clubs.

Well a lot of the white girls in the troupe frequented these clubs and didn't believe me.

With a little coaxing we started out on our way to Rush Street and a night of fun and celebration.

No one mentioned my concerns anymore even though I'm sure it was lurking in the back of some of our minds.

I dropped off all the people riding with me at the door to look for a parking space and upon returning I attempted to enter the club and was told I was not welcome.

After about 20 minutes or so some of the girls from the troupe came to the door looking for me only to see me on the curb in front of the building.

At first there was this look of bewilderment on their faces that quickly changed to anger.

My friends then began to lash out at the bouncers for refusing to let me in and also how they had no idea THAT was the way they were doing business. Ha!!!

The bouncers were overwhelmed and asked me to come in and I joined the rest of the troupe inside the club.

But something was very different.

When everyone found out what had taken me so long it seemed like no one wanted to celebrate anymore.

Everyone seemed sad.

Perhaps because the world they thought they knew well came crashing down around them in that instant. :0(

That is perhaps why we reject change so much. We are comfortable where we are and here comes the big change.

Now it is time to adapt.

Well to that I say so what!!!!

My whole life has been about change and adaptation or better yet "plan B."

The troupe was pretty sad and even though it was proven that I was accurate and they were merely unaware, it wasn't about being accurate at that time.

You see these were my friends, and they were hurting inside from perhaps a myriad of things.

Maybe they were ashamed that they unknowingly promoted and even frequented establishments like that.

Perhaps they felt disgust that this sort of nonsense still existed and last but not least they could have felt betrayed by the club.

To learn the bouncers who welcomed them into these clubs innocently on sooo many different occasions only to slam the door behind them when a black guy showed up could be somewhat SHOCKING. Ha!!!

A behavior that they obviously would not condone, but try to tell the black guys standing outside that my girls aren't racist and they may reply, "Then why do they party there?"

The answer I pray is…that they don't know.

Anyway, not wanting to allow that night to become a total disaster I reassured everyone that it was no big deal and the way to get back at the establishment was for us to have a good time anyway.

Oh yeah, and for all the white girls to come home with me. Ha!!!

Just kidding…or am I?

After all this was a modeling troupe with some beautiful women in the group.

Seriously though, that was a perfect example of having to make a change at the drop of a hat aka plan B.

So remember the next time you're in a club in Chicagoland and you don't see any black guys you may want to ask yourself, "What gives?"

Getting back to ending racism, it was obvious that the models were walking around with blinders on about how cruel the world is.

There's nothing wrong with that because why should we ALWAYS be on the offensive?

It's stupid that black guys have to have a list of places that are okay to frequent and a list of places that are off limits. Ha!!!!

It is even more pitiful that an owner can convince someone to pick and choose its clientele based on his or her skin color and for the numbskull to actually follow that direction.

In other words I'm your boss and I want you to work at my hot dog stand. However I give you explicit instructions not to let any white people ever enjoy the succulent juices of my hot dog and refuse them service.

Does that sound right??? Ha!!!

As someone seeking employment would you readily work there? Hmmmmm???

Does that owner need to be reported?

How many stories have we heard about human resource departments not considering employing someone because their name is too ethnic or they show up and to their surprise Tony Smith is a black dude, and another personal friend of mine by the way? Ha!!!

Now, again, I don't want to appear contradictory but I will quote my father again and say, "I don't discriminate because I know how some black people are!"

In other words, black people can be jerks too, which is my point, that "content of their character" thing can go a long way with making the world a better place to live in.

We don't put enough effort toward important things, settling for bad information because we are too lazy to investigate for ourselves or just following orders like the stupid bouncers of the world keeping the scary black guys out of the country clubs and night clubs across the tracks.

Is it me or doesn't it seem like the dummies are the bouncers and the like who would fall for such foolishness and actually try to execute the nefarious orders?

These guys will jump off of that infamous bridge when instructed but how about ordering them to not be a simpleton?

In other words I order you to not be a racist! Will I be met with another war?

If so why?

Are we that adverse to new information?

Yeah there's a war going on like in desert storm but this one's on the streets in front of my home in Jena, Louisiana.

I'll be glad when good people stop-allowing bad people to use them and end up ultimately victimizing themselves.

We all know the difference between right and wrong as children and sitting under a shady tree is no reason for war, at least not until somebody goes putting a noose on the tree to send some sort of sick message.

Why can't everyone sit under the stupid tree and be quiet.

I got news for you, it ain't your tree anyway it belongs to 'you know who.' Ha!!!!!

How many flash floods, fires, earthquakes or Katrina's will it take before we figure out 'you know who' might be a little disgusted with our behavior.

Settle down Pat Robertson....;0) Ha!!!!

You don't have to hit me over the head with another war for me to get the message; it is time for a change.

You know I was watching a documentary about a bunch of wannabe racists called the Skinheads and how they formed a record company to promote and sell songs about hate.

The owners of the company were proud of their efforts and how their sales rose from 7000 copies to 11,000 copies and who knows how many copies they're selling these days.

Well I want to also declare war on that record company and any more like that.

If a record company can sell 11,000 copies of hatred then

I want 111,000,000 people to support this songbook about LOVE.

I want to send a message to all bigots that no matter how hard they try to RUSH and promote ignorance their FOXy numbers will never be relevant.

I have faith that nice guys don't always have to finish last. Ha!!!!

All my life I have had to struggle with just falling short of a goal I would set for myself. Goals based on doing the right things creatively and spiritually where the only potential of damage would only affect myself if things didn't work out.

Well unfortunately I became an expert at accepting failure.

Even though I wrote a great song called Jack'n The Beanstalk and Michael Jackson even came up with the same idea, nothing ever became of that dream.

Now I'm sure Michael Jackson has way more success stories than I can possibly imagine so when his desire to do a project didn't work out it wouldn't have been devastating like it can for a guy like me. RIP King of Pop.

Or when our modeling troupe had to break up arguably due to mismanagement only to be followed up by the rise and fall of "All Tall" a singing group I put together with some guys that actually were all tall.

We were zeroing in on our style when one of the main members left the 3-man group to pursue other things crushing my spirit to keep on reaching out to the world.

And how can I not mention all the failed attempts at relationships that a young lady or I would mess up.

To me life was what seemed like a never-ending cycle of disappointment where it is just a matter of time before you join the ranks of the quitters.

Then here comes "The New Style Players" to the rescue and even though we experienced some of the same problems, if not worse, I managed to stay positive no matter what ordeals we encountered and maintained the vision of the group.

Ha!!!!

I know these songs can reach people; they just have to be heard on a level playing field and let people be the judge. Well here I am, come and take me.

I am putting myself out here to be judged.

I don't have a dream team like Johnnie Cochran for my defense it's just me and my boys, NSP, and a little something we call Hip Hopera.

There may be some haters…I mean people who feel these recordings could have been produced a lot better which is also why I have another hope. A hope that professional artists will cover some of these songs and give them their just desserts via say a Walt Disney perhaps as a Broadway musical.

Don't you hear Sir Elton John jamming LIES with Prince singing duet and playing an awesome lead guitar part? How about Ne-Yo or Usher singing "Just Can't Live My Life Alone?"

I can hear it just as plain as day. Ha!!!!

Anyway, like all wars I just want this war on nonsense to end with as little bloodshed as quickly and quietly as possible.

Like the song "WARS," says, "stop pretending nobody cares, unless you got people over there," then it will really be a better day. Ha!!!

NO MORE

You don't know me
I don't know you
But we both know
That one thing is true

If we believe
One day we'll see
Hold on to faith
No more greed

No more lying
No more pain
No more crying
Tears like rain

No more hiding
From the truth
No more crying
Cause it's up to you

No more…we need equal basis
No more…no more naming races
No more…no more racist faces
No more…for our point in case is…No more

No more…if you really want it
No more…you can get it
No more…but cha got to stay on it
No more…never quit it

Heyyyyy Shakira…..;0) Ha!!

Chapter 10

What's up New Style?

Nowadays it is hard for us to trust people. In today's society it appears that most people will only do things with an ulterior motive, the old "what's in it for me?" factor.

Well this songbook isn't that much different, only I want the world to benefit from this experience, not ME individually.

I feel if we can get to a place, like that day at Oprah Winfrey's studio for the workshop on racism, the world, without a doubt, will be a better place.

There were so many different cultures that day socializing in harmony and peace.

Laughter and goodwill were all that was on anyone's mind that day. All fears were erased thanks to the documentary, workshop, and the discussions that followed.

Not to mention the WILL of the people who were there, recognizing that a change in attitude was and is warranted, and a drive to initiate that change was evident thereafter.

Where there's a will there's a way. Ha!!!

Yes we can!!!

See, in the studio, that day, the audience all knew one thing that's true.

There's no more room for lying and the pain.

It's time to come together and take responsibility for our current actions, the previous actions of our ancestors, and to begin to repair the damages of discrimination that continue to haunt us today for our future's sake.

The reason I want this song "No More" delivered in various languages is so people will begin to see, hear and totally understand HOW MUCH we need each other all over the world and stop fighting.

Don't listen to that 'beware' rhetoric about other cultures and their so-called stereotypes. How many jerks do you know in your own race??

Nobel Peace Prize winner President Obama gets ridiculed for trying to build international bridges apparently it is supposed to come off as appearing weak…Ha!!!

People deserve a chance to be proven a jerk, don't you think?

I met a guy, John, who told me about how his father had gotten beaten up by some black guys, just because he was white, after Martin Luther King Jr. was assassinated during the riots.

True, sometimes our fears ring true about groups of people, and THAT'S what gets me so angry sometimes.

Don't prove the racist right!!

We fall from grace when we choose to go down the wrong road, for example, selling illegal drugs or beating up John's father.

How can we faithfully argue for equality if every time you turn around somebody is acting like a bad apple? Ha!!!

I remember when the first O.J. Simpson thing was just starting up.

I was still a Chicago Firefighter and Dionne Warwick had just gone off television saying how she knew O.J. was innocent.

Well, I was chiming in like a choirboy that he was innocent and the police didn't know what they were talking about.

The next work-day was when O.J. was in that infamous white Ford Bronco, 'looking' guiltier than Richard Simmons at a Dunkin Donut doughnut shop around 3am with a hat, sunglasses and a trench coat on.

A fellow firefighter inquired, "What do you have to say now Bahb?"

Even though he was found not guilty thanks to the efforts of Johnnie Cochran's team, that day in the Bronco, he was embarrassing me and I don't even know him.

When it's time for us to decide whether or not to behave with dignity or with ethics, it shouldn't be a tug of war. It should be easy, but as they say, it's easier to do the wrong thing than it is to do the right thing. Ha!!!

No more!!!!!

Hold on to faith, no more greed. It's all the same, no matter what language it's spoken in. We all know the difference between right and wrong, I don't care if you're from Antarctica.

That's cold. Ha!!!!

The Most High planned for us all to figure out how to get along. If not he wouldn't have put us here together in the first place. That's why I am perplexed by all this war all over the place.

True, I live and grew up in America, but the concept of war is still a very hard sell for me to accept.

I don't understand why people fight over land, religion or even wealth.

Remember to me money is nothing more than green pieces of paper for the most part.

To me, NOTHING is worth killing over. Especially when the argument stems from religious beliefs or money. Ha!!!

How can you base fighting over religious beliefs? That's a huge oxymoron. My God would be ashamed of our ignorance.

To me, it better be an awfully good reason to go to war over something. Remember for every action there is a re-action.

I know 9/11 got us Americans all fired up to want revenge,

but perhaps we should have delved more into what prompted that extraordinary behavior in the first place.

I'm not saying it could possibly ever be justified, murdering that many innocent Americans. But to target the innocents, my first big question was why?

Bin Laden apparently is too busy hiding to elaborate on the rationale behind it, if he truly was responsible, because correct me if I'm wrong, did he ever own up to being the genius behind 9/11??? Give me more than a sound bite.

This goes back to my complaint about these insurgents chopping off innocent's heads with their faces all covered up.

If you are so proud and patriotic why are you hiding your face? Ha!!!

So, to Mr. Laden, if you did it then say so, at least we knew Adolph Hitler was calling all the shots cause he didn't hide who he was or what he was trying to do.

Apparently Hitler thought he was justified for his behavior because he didn't wear a mask.

It is still somewhat of a mystery to me, yes or no, concretely, who to credit for 9/11.

Doesn't matter, The Most High knows who you are, and whoever it is will have to be held accountable. I'm sure HE won't be pleased with that sort of behavior. Ha!!!!

If you really believe in paradise then hold onto faith. There's an old expression, " It's going to get greater, later."

The Most High has a plan for everybody.

Who are we to question His will?

As horrible as it was for me and everyone else close to 9/11, we have to TRUST His plan for us and KNOW there was a reason for that to happen to us.

One thing about 9/11, it definitely brought Americans closer together.

There truly was an undeniable bonding across the United States after 9/11 that, whoever caused it, was not anticipating that love bug I'm sure.

We as people were created in The Most High's image and before the curse of Adam and Eve, we were strong, obedient people.

Now we're all messed up with selfishness and superiority complexes.

I know that I am not better than anyone else on this planet, but on the same note, there isn't anyone better than me, with the ....possible exception of my boys Jamie Mayes, Jamie Shelton, Greg, Brian and Charlie H., Warren McBride, David Ireland, Dana Marberry, Frank Long, Lester McCarrol, David Jackson, Francisco "Boo" Hardy, and my Big Brother Pastor Anthony Jenkins Ha!!!!

My point is these mixed up ways of thinking is probably why all this confusion started in the first place, somebody believing they were BETTER than somebody else and then carrying it to an extreme.

Well I really don't want any more confusion in the land and I know we can get to that point of agreement, I got to stay on it, and I promise that I'll never quit it.

No more.

Ha!!!!

GONNA BE A BETTER DAY

Everyday and every minute that I'm awake
Feel the pain
Why we got to keep on paying for the same mistakes
Wonder what I'm living for
Reach for the ceiling or the floor
Got to be a better day

Sometimes I wonder what was on my mind
That's why (always)
I look at my life through open eyes
Like grand momma used to say
It's gonna be a better day
But you got to believe it

Day gonna be better
Day gonna be fine
Day gonna be better always
Tomorrows on my mind
Day gonna be better for you and me (you'll see)

Not by myself (gonna need somebody)
Who'll take every breath
Until nothing else is left
Help from the rich poor weak and strong
As long as we can all get along
It'll be a better day

From now on
I promise that I'll dedicate and be strong
Try to help someone along their way
I don't care who's right or wrong
That's why we had to make this song
Because we want to SEE a better day

Chapter 11

Okay New Style

Here we are, after the madness. I guess we all CAN just get along. Like grandmamma used to say, it's gonna be a better day.

Call me optimistic, gullible, or just a dreamer but I do believe that when the world strives for higher levels of education, formal and or otherwise, and we are all able to register and vote with intelligence, racism will be defeated.

There's no need for society to keep paying for the same mistakes of past and current racist idealists.

It's gonna be a better day. But, you got to believe it.

I know, it's hard to forget about the past atrocities that different cultures have had to endure throughout history. But there has to come a day when we should attempt to forgive and forget the past, in order for us to move forward with our lives, together, on this earth. Ha!!!!!

Let's make a conscious effort to better the world today and every day. It's the only earth we've got so we might as well party together every once and a while.

I'm not saying go out and marry someone from a different race to show your sincerity, just don't NOT meet or marry somebody simply because of his or her race.

To each his own. Like I said, "There's plenty of ugly to go around." The Lord doesn't discriminate. Ha!!!!

You know, speaking of ugly, there is more than one kind of ugly. It doesn't necessarily have to describe a physical ugliness, how about an ugly spirit!! How about a person just acting ugly?

We know 'you know who' don't like ugly.

On the flip side, when we do the right thing, the world is a beautiful place to be. If it's going to be a better day, it's going to take everyone's help, not just me. Help from the rich, poor, weak and strong, and then it will be a better day.

I remember that workshop on racism at the Oprah Winfrey show and what the atmosphere was like after a few hours were well spent discussing the differences about being different.

There wasn't any animosity; it was more like a love fest.

People were truly comfortable together. It was as if a heavy weight had been lifted off everyone's shoulders.

As if to say, it is okay to mingle with each other without feeling threatened.

How about a reunion Ms. Winfrey? Hello!!!!

Warning, don't get carried away with reaching out to others. Remember, there are plenty of jerks in all-different colors.

Plenty of people out there we SHOULD avoid Debra. Use your best judgment in your decision making process about who to hang out with.

First impressions last a long time. Ha!!!

You know, it seems when the old style racist would have a baby and while the babies were infants they wouldn't care about the future racist infant child mingling with different races as a way to perhaps baby-sit the child.

You know, give them someone to play with, keep them quiet, or under control because a baby will even rattle a racist.

Then once the racist infant would reach a certain age, the line would be clearly drawn to separate themselves from the other race socially for the rest of their lives.

It was probably sad to the infant in the beginning to be separated, but later on it would perhaps be soon forgotten about those infantile friendships or alliances with brown people.

I want us all to go back to that childlike way of life. When all we wanted was someone to play with.

Do you remember those days?

I hope so because I do.

I'm reminded of it everytime I see a child's face.

Originally, when I went to Ms. Winfrey's workshop show, I had big dreams and ambitions that I was going to jump-start my movement to try to make the world a better place. Ha!!!!

That was several years ago.

I also thought writing these and other songs would make me well received in the music industry, since it was for a good cause. Double Ha!!!

Yeah right.

It's been a long haul putting this project together and the way my luck goes I'll probably pass away before this songbook becomes the success I imagine.

I have been frustrated time and time again trying to make an impact on a large scale, only to keep seeing my great ideas pop up via other celebrities.

For example actor Robert Townsend used the word Hip-Hopera for his re-production of Carmen starring Beyonce Knowles. And Michael Jackson produced my idea for "Jack'n the Beanstalk". The Fireman song wasn't a good idea until after 9/11. Now there's a new found respect for the risks taken by firefighters. Even the rapper Lil Wayne has "The Fireman" in his catalogue of songs.

There are countless other songs that combine spirituality with a good beat that you can dance to, in the New Style Hip Hopera tradition. Ha!!!

Of course, to me, there was always something missing from these formulas....ME!!!!

It was enough to make a guy want to give up altogether on his dreams of a better place "before I die."

I could even say that people were stifling me along the way, left and right, through deceit and trickery, almost breaking me down to a mere morsel of a man.

Through it all I managed to hold on to faith and believe that one-day, one way or another, I was going to be able to expose the world to what I had to say ANYWAY.

It's okay to believe you have a little talent, but nothing beats a little recognition for those efforts every once in a while.

Am I silly?

Am I spoiled?

Am I delirious?

I hope not!

I also hope it doesn't stop here with this songbook. Ha!!!!!

Why not take this energy to another level world?

From here, why not focus more on things like recycling and the environment for example?

I can't stress enough about our society's need to reach for higher levels of education to reap the multiple benefits that will evolve from learning, not just ending racism.

What about black dudes getting their hair lined in the front so much, unaware that it likely will result in early baldness?

Stop doing that! Ha!!!!

Amen brot...Huh..."What did he say????"

Barbers across America unite; we black dudes look crazy to me with that darned line across our foreheads.

Are black male foreheads getting bigger??

Hey, always leave em' laughing.

It's gonna be a better day.

Oh yeah...I almost forgot......Ha!!!!

Printed in the United States
By Bookmasters